W9-BCQ-494

HOME PLATE

FROM HOT DOGS TO HAUTE CUISINE

*This book is dedicated
to the memory of everyone's first game.*

Home Plate is the result of the time, talent and dedication
of many gifted professionals.

Special thanks to:

Chef Rolf Baumann, who gently coached and encouraged his culinary team,
at times cooking with one hand and answering e-mail with the other.

Master Chef Roland Henin and Chef Beth Brown for testing and editing every recipe,
and for offering moral support to the sports chefs.

Chef Eric Borgia and our all-star chefs at Delaware North Companies Sportservice
athletic and entertainment venues throughout North America.

Our client and partner at the Reno-Sparks Convention Center for the use of the facilities and kitchens.

Our client and partner at San Diego's PETCO Park for the use of kitchens and the playing field.

Mary Burich, for bringing the vision of *Home Plate* to life.

Christopher Whitcomb, who kept the project on track by handling seemingly endless details flawlessly.

The Jacobs family – past and present – for comprehending and embracing
the most powerful force on Earth: possibility.

Special Limited Edition

Second Edition

Copyright © 2007 Delaware North Companies

All rights reserved. No portion of this book may be reproduced — mechanically, electronically,

or by any means, including photocopying — without the written permission of the publisher.

ISBN: (13) 978-0-9790917-0-4

(10) 0-9790917-0-5

Design by Wynne Creative Group

Photography by Emily Nathan

Printed in China

For additional information or to visit us at more than 150 locations worldwide, contact:

Wendy Watkins, vice president of corporate communication and marketing; or Mary Burich, editor.

For information about Sportservice, contact: Rick Abramson, president; Richard Dobransky,

vice president of food and beverage; Barry Freilicher, vice president of business development.

Any trademarks, service marks, trade names, slogans, designs, or logos ("IP") appearing in this

publication that are not the property of Delaware North Companies, Inc. or its subsidiaries are the

property of and are owned by third parties. The inclusion of such third-party IP in this publication

is not, and should not be construed as an endorsement, implied sponsorship or implied affiliation

with Delaware North Companies, Inc. or its subsidiaries.

Delaware North Companies, 40 Fountain Plaza, Buffalo, New York 14202-2285

716-858-5000

DelawareNorth.com

TABLE OF CONTENTS

4

EXECUTIVE CHEF ROLF BAUMANN

With a Blackberry in one hand and a whisk in the other, Rolf Baumann is able to do the two things he does best: stay in touch with his chefs and cook. Both are essential, he maintains, imparting a philosophy that is well on its way to leaving a mark on the longest standing culinary operation in the sports industry.

"The chefs know they can call me anytime with a question or to ask advice," he says. And pointing to the cell phone that is always in his hip pocket, he adds, "I couldn't keep up any other way."

Talented, good-humored and having seemingly boundless energy, one advantage Chef Rolf doesn't have is spare time. He is on planes and in hotel rooms more often than he is home. And when he walks the concourses of the Delaware North Companies Sportservice locations whose kitchens he oversees, it is with a gait that is quick and deliberate.

A culinary Olympian with other international honors and more than 25 medals to his credit, Chef Rolf is German-born and -bred. His early days were spent at his grandmother's side, where he watched her cook for visitors of the guesthouse she ran. At 14, he left home to begin a three-year culinary apprenticeship, which led him to positions in various restaurants in Heilbronn, Germany. He came to the United States in 1984 to serve as a pastry chef for a major hotel in Dallas, and from there, went to Hilton Head, South Carolina; and to Little Rock, Arkansas.

When he was a young 30-something, he joined Sportservice as the executive chef for Busch Stadium in St. Louis. There he was responsible for all premium dining, restaurants and concessions. Now it's just one of the dozens of famous kitchens he routinely works in, striving always to please hungry and increasingly discerning fans.

"People want choices," he says. "They want to know they have the option of something different."

But not just different. Chef Rolf maintains that better must be part of the mix as well. "We have to be prepared to give fans more variety, but the food has to be high quality," he says. And then he's off. The phone is ringing.

OUR COMPLIMENTS
TO THE CHEFS

The recipes that fill the pages of *Home Plate* represent some of the most sought-after dishes from the sporting and entertainment venues where Delaware North Companies Sportservice is pleased to operate. From the company-owned TD Banknorth Garden in Boston to Rexall Place in Edmonton to PETCO Park in San Diego and many locations in between, there are regional and venue favorites, and chefs' specialties to please every palate.

We understand you won't be serving 50,000 at your gathering, so each recipe was edited and tested for home use by us. Joining us from The Ahwahnee in Yosemite National Park was Chef Beth Brown, who tested all of the recipes in the company's earlier volume, *Pathways to Plate*.

The photographed dishes were prepared by us in the kitchen of PETCO Park's SONY Dugout Club thanks to the generosity and hospitality of the San Diego Padres. What you see is what you get. Nothing was used to enhance the presentation or to substitute for a genuine food item. Had we even considered it, we're convinced our chefs wouldn't have stood for it.

In the end, you'll find a wide array of items that are typical of the fare you'll find at our venues. From easy to difficult; from casual to elegant. Don't be surprised if your guests gravitate toward lip-smacking, but unassuming, Fried Cookie Dough and Buffalo-Style Chicken Wings even though you're as proud as can be of your Prosciutto and Spinach Rotol and Avocado Crema Fresca.

Our chefs had full control over the recipes they submitted, which is as it should be. No one knows the tastes and preferences of a location's guests better than the person who cooks for them. It was a lot of fun for us to see the dishes coming in and to make all of them. I think it's safe to say we have some new favorites to make at home.

We hope you will, too. But first, help us celebrate the wonderful and indivisible relationship between food and sports, and the work of the culinary team we believe is the best in the business.

Rolf Baumann, CEC

Roland Henin, CMC

FAN FAVORITES

Once upon a time, food and drinks weren't sold at sporting venues.

Imagine what those contests were like. No hot dogs, no beer vendors, nary a peanut. If you got hungry or bored, you stayed hungry or bored. If you were treating friends or business associates to an afternoon out, you hoped they wouldn't be hungry or bored.

Kind of like the dark ages. At least for those who work to uphold the traditions of Delaware North Companies Sportservice, the first sporting concessions company in America.

Back in 1915, food at the stadium was a novel idea, and one born of necessity. At least for its birth mothers – or fathers – as they were.

The three Jacobs brothers figured it out before anyone else. When you're sitting in the sun for hours, your lips tend to get dry; your stomach begins to rumble. So much so, there's a likelihood you'll pony up to alleviate either or both. And that doesn't even begin to scratch the surface of the near mystical relationship humans have with their chow.

It was the perfect initiative to replace the income the Jacobses lost when theaters – their bread and butter – closed down in the summer because of the oppressive heat in non-air-conditioned buildings. Jersey City had the first Sportservice concessions. Tiger Stadium in 1930 was the first major league park in the company's portfolio.

Not that the menu compared with today's fare, mind you. Even a few decades ago, Rick Abramson recalls cheese sandwiches being de rigueur at places like Milwaukee's County Stadium, where he cut his teeth. And he's not talking about a four-cheese panini with tomato and olive pesto. White bread. And a slice of orange cheese. The oranger the better.

He is the begetter of Sportservice's famous Secret Stadium Sauce and the current president of the company he began hawking food for when he was in his teens.

The fateful day came in the early '70s. "We were running out of barbecue sauce," he says. "So I doctored up some ketchup."

Did it catch on? "Most people who buy a brat at Miller Park today [by the way, there are scads of them] adorn it with the private-label condiment," says Rick.

Sportscaster Bob Costas is willing to put a Sportservice bratwurst with Secret Stadium Sauce up against feed from any other ballpark. Still, the sensation never caught on outside Milwaukee. Perhaps because when it comes to regional specialties, there are enough bragging rights to go around. There's no need to copy other cities' ideas. In other words, Brewers fans can stand up and be counted, but they won't be alone.

Case in point: You could fill the stands of virtually every major sporting venue with hot dog bigots alone. Grilled, steamed, boiled? All-pork, all-beef, a combination of the two, kosher? Not to mention buns and toppings.

U.S. Cellular Field in Chicago serves its frankfurters sans ketchup (if you must have it, put it on your French fries, White Sox fans maintain), but with neon-green relish and on a poppy-seed bun. PETCO Park gives its version a decidedly south-of-the-border twist. The kind of mustard you use in Cleveland — Stadium or Bertman's — will depend on whether you're watching the Indians or the Browns.

The unpretentious link consistently outsells hamburgers and is top dog everywhere except Miller Park, where the brat is king. The lowly peanut is the best-selling fan favorite bar none, but nachos have been moving up in the world, nudging out popcorn for second place.

Sportservice serves more of the chips-and-cheese snack at Busch Stadium than at any other venue, and yet manages to satisfy Cardinals fans' appetites for other specialties like St. Louis Toasted Ravioli and handmade pretzels. Ever wonder why Cincinnati Reds spectators walk around eating food out of paper bags? Order Fried Cookie Dough and you'll have your answer.

Contemporary fans are arguably better educated, wealthier and more sophisticated than their predecessors. Is it despite that or because of it that they are quick to treat themselves to food that's just plain good and fun? "It's the 80/20 rule when you're talking about fine dining versus concessions," Rick says. "Most people go for the tried-and-true offerings."

Which just goes to prove, yet again, what Humphrey Bogart once said: "A hot dog at the ballpark is better than steak at the Ritz."

BOSTON

TD Banknorth Garden

There aren't many places in the world like TD Banknorth Garden. Or should we say, "the Gah-den."

The official home base of Delaware North Companies' Boston operations houses the NHL's Boston Bruins, the NBA's Boston Celtics and the National Lacrosse League's newest expansion team. However, what makes this facility unlike any other is its combination of state-of-the-art technology and sports history.

The successor to the original Boston Garden, TD Banknorth Garden offers fans a chance to remember the successes of past Bruins and Celtics championships. Numerous exhibits pay tribute to such hockey greats as Bobby Orr, Phil Esposito and Ray Bourque. Basketball fans can conjure up memories of Larry Bird and Bill Russell as they work their way through the arena.

Arguably one of the best venues of its kind in the world, the Garden is a year-round facility with seats for 19,600 fans. In addition to renowned sporting events, the Garden has often been called upon to hold major events such as the 2004 Democratic National Convention and the 1996 NHL All-Star Game.

With an unparalleled list of past events on its resumé, TD Banknorth Garden is proud of its history, but focused on its future. Now equipped with such fine dining restaurants as Banners and sports clubs like Legends, the stadium combines great food with great experiences to make it a total package.

Bock Beer Poached Shrimp

Bock is a German beer whose name means "goat." Some say that's due to the "kick" bock drinkers get soon after raising a stein of the strong lager to their lips. Either way, poaching shrimp in the hearty brew will be a welcome surprise. Our chefs insist the shrimp are perfect by themselves, but if you desire, cocktail or dipping sauce can accompany them.

Prep time: 45 minutes
Cook time: 35 minutes
Yields: 6 servings

24 peeled and cleaned shrimp
 (16 to 20 per pound)
1 quart shrimp stock or seafood broth
 (prepared stock can be substituted)
2 bottles bock beer

1 cup white wine
1/4 cup chopped lemon grass
1 tablespoon chopped, fresh ginger
2 tablespoons Tabasco sauce
2 bay leaves

1 bunch curly parsley
Salt to taste
Ground black pepper to taste
1 lemon

Place each shrimp on a 7-inch wood skewer, tail first, so it resembles a satay. Refrigerate. Place all remaining ingredients (except lemon) in a 2- to 3-quart saucepan and bring to a simmer for 20 minutes. Place shrimp skewers in simmering stock for 8 to 10 minutes.

Remove shrimp from stock and let cool for 10 minutes. Place in refrigerator until ready to serve. Squeeze lemon juice over shrimp before serving.

New England Clam Chowder

While New England Clam Chowder is famous around the globe, there's nothing like enjoying it in its home state. This easy-to-follow recipe lets you bring a little bit of Boston into your kitchen.

Prep time: 30 minutes
Cook time: 50 minutes
Yields: 8 (1-cup) servings

5 pounds cherry stone clams or quahogs
  (can also use canned clams)
1 1/2 quarts fish stock (or water)
4 ounces diced and smoked bacon*
4 ounces diced and skinned salt pork*

3 medium peeled and diced Idaho potatoes*
4 washed and diced celery stalks*
1 small, diced Spanish onion*
1 1/2 peeled and smashed garlic cloves
1 1/2 bay leaves

3 picked and chopped thyme sprigs
2 cups heavy cream
1 bunch minced chives

Wash all of the clams under cold running water. Place stock or water into a large stockpot. Add washed clams to the stockpot. Bring to a simmer over medium heat. Cover and cook 15 minutes or until all the clams have opened. Remove all the clams, discard the ones that have not opened and reserve the rest. Strain the liquid to remove any sand resulting from the clams, and place the strained liquid back in the stockpot.

Place diced bacon and salt pork in a heavy-bottom saucepan and begin to render over medium-low heat. When salt pork and bacon are crisp, remove from pot using a slotted spoon. Discard the pieces or save and add to the soup at the end.

Add one of the diced potatoes, two of the celery stalks, onion and garlic to the rendered fat. Add the stock and bring to a simmer. Cook for 15 minutes or until the potatoes are tender.

While the stock is cooking, remove clams from the shells and chop. Reserve the chopped clams until needed.

Once the vegetables are tender, place the simmering stock into a food processor or blender and carefully purée until smooth. Place the smooth mixture back into the saucepan. Add the remaining potatoes and celery, along with the bay leaves and thyme sprigs. Bring up to a simmer and cook until the potatoes are tender.

Add the cream and the chopped clams to the soup and simmer 5 minutes longer or until cream is heated through.

Season with salt and pepper, sprinkle some of the crackling on top if desired, garnish with chives and serve hot.

* Dicing should yield 1/4 -inch pieces.

Chilled Cucumber and Apple Fresca Soup

A cool, savory blend of fruit and vegetables, this dish is perfect for hot summer months. Add lobster or crab meat to give this wonderful soup even more flair.

Prep time: 45 minutes
Yields: 8 (8-ounce) servings

1 cup whole milk

6 peeled and cored Granny Smith apples

1/4 diced yellow onion*

1 seeded and diced green bell pepper*

1 1/2 cups peeled, seeded and diced
   English cucumber*

3 ounces white grape juice concentrate

1 cup sour cream

2 cups buttermilk

2 tablespoons finely chopped parsley

Salt to taste

Ground black pepper to taste

Minced chives or green onions for garnish,
   if desired

To prevent milk from curdling when it is combined with the vegetables, place it in a small saucepan and bring to a boil over medium heat. Set milk aside to cool.

Juice apples, onion, green pepper, and one-half of the cucumber in a bar blender with half of the grape juice concentrate and a small amount of the milk. Liquefy the solids with as little liquid as possible in order to get a fine blend.

Once all solids are puréed to a very fine, smooth consistency, whisk in remaining juice, milk, buttermilk and sour cream until completely incorporated. Mix in remaining cucumber and parsley.

Season with salt and pepper to taste. Chill completely. Freeze soup tureen for service. Garnish with chives or green onions.

* Dicing should yield 1/4-inch pieces.

Commonly referred to as a vegetable, in botanical terms, a cucumber is the fruit of a vine, and thus, is technically grouped with sweeter family members like apples, pears and berries. Considered a native plant of India, cucumbers were cultivated for more than 3,000 years in western Asia and gradually introduced to parts of Europe by the Romans. As evidence of their ancient origins, cucumbers are mentioned in the Old Testament.

New England Lobster Roll

Nothing says New England like lobster, and this classic dish has been known to spark a debate about where to get the biggest and best. Our chef keeps his recipe simple, letting the flavor and texture of the fresh seafood speak for themselves.

Prep time: 15 minutes
Yields: 4 servings

1 pound fresh Maine lobster meat (from tail, claw and knuckle)	1 cup mayonnaise*	Ground black pepper to taste
1/2 lemon	1 peeled and diced rib of celery	12 chiffonade-cut lettuce leaves**
	Salt to taste	4 New England-style rolls

Chop lobster meat in medium to large pieces and place in a chilled bowl.

Squeeze lemon and mix juice with mayonnaise. Add lemon mayonnaise to lobster, followed by the diced celery. Fold together. Add salt and pepper to taste.

Place lettuce on the bottom half of each roll and top with lobster.

Serve immediately.

Note: Rolls can be toasted before placing lobster mixture in them.

*Mayonnaise can be adjusted to taste. One cup will result in a heavy mixture.
**Chiffonade means to cut into thin strips.

The generic term lobster generally refers to the American or Maine version of the crustacean that lives in the cold, shallow waters of the North Atlantic. Providing they can elude natural predators such as codfish, flounder and haddock, lobsters can live up to 100 years, continually growing to a weight of as much as 40 pounds.

Wild Mushroom Pork Belly Risotto

A wonderful twist for pork lovers, this dish's combination of flavors is sure to please any pallet. Also a visual delight, this recipe will keep family members and guests alike coming back for more.

Prep time (Braised Pork Belly): 2 hours, 20 minutes
Prep time (Risotto): 40 minutes
Yields: 6 servings

FOR THE BRAISED PORK BELLY

2 tablespoons olive oil

1 pound pork belly

1 cup white wine

1 cup diced carrots*

1 cup diced celery*

1 cup diced onion*

1 sprig thyme

1 bay leaf

1 quart water

FOR THE WILD MUSHROOM RISOTTO

1/4 cup olive oil

1 cup cleaned, trimmed and sliced chanterelle
    mushrooms (can use any mushroom)**

1 cup cleaned, trimmed and sliced shiitake mushrooms**

2/3 cup cognac or brandy

3/4 cup heavy cream

4 cups chicken stock (can substitute chicken broth
    or any canned chicken stock)

2 cups pork stock from braising pork belly liquid

1 tablespoon unsalted butter

4 peeled and minced medium shallots

1 3/4 cups arborio rice

1/3 cup grated Parmesan cheese

Salt to taste

Ground black pepper to taste

2 tablespoons chopped parsley

For the Braised Pork Belly

Preheat oven to 300° F.

Heat olive oil in medium skillet over medium-high heat. Sear pork for 4 minutes on each side.

Remove pork and deglaze pan with white wine.

Add all of the vegetables, thyme and bay leaf.

Add water and simmer for 10 minutes.

Place pork with all ingredients into a roasting pan. Cover with plastic wrap, followed by aluminum foil. Braise for 2 hours or until fork tender.

When tender, keep pork warm with 1/2 cup stock. Strain and reserve remaining liquid for risotto.

For the Wild Mushroom Risotto

Place 2 tablespoons of olive oil in a medium skillet over medium-high heat. Add mushrooms and sauté approximately 5 minutes. Add cognac and bring to a boil. Cook for 3 to 4 minutes or until liquid is reduced by half. Lower heat to medium, add cream and simmer 5 minutes. Remove skillet from heat and set aside.

Bring chicken and pork stocks to a simmer in a saucepan.

In a deep, medium saucepan, heat remaining oil. Add butter and shallots, and cook for 2 minutes or until soft. Add rice and stir to coat with oil and butter. Add simmering stock 1/2 cup at a time, stirring enough to keep rice from sticking to the pan. Wait until the stock is almost absorbed before adding next 1/2 cup. The process will take 20 minutes. The rice should be just cooked and slightly chewy.

Stir in mushroom mixture and the Parmesan cheese. Season to taste with salt and pepper. Serve risotto with braised pork belly. Garnish with chopped parsley.

*Dicing should yield 1/4-inch pieces.
**Slicing should yield 1/2-inch pieces.

BUFFALO

HSBC Arena

HSBC Arena in downtown Buffalo pretty much does it all.

The official home of the Buffalo Sabres and the National Lacrosse League's Buffalo Bandits, the venue also hosts concerts, ice shows and a good deal of other entertainment that stops in Buffalo. The first two rounds of the 2000, 2004 and 2007 NCAA Division I Men's Basketball Championship and the 2003 Frozen Four Division I Men's Ice Hockey Championship gave the arena an opportunity to shine for the nation.

Make no mistake: This is a sports town. And the Buffalo Sabres have provided enough drama of late to keep the tradition alive and well. The NHL franchise made runs to the Eastern Conference Finals in the 2005-2006 and 2006-2007 seasons, and in 2006, the team set the record for most consecutive wins by bagging its first 10 games.

Fans loved every minute of it, too. They enjoyed the games from the friendly confines of HSBC Arena. Outfitted with the Pepsi Headlines Sports Bar, the Harbour Club and the Greater Buffalo Sports Hall of Fame, the arena is a place where Buffalo fans feel at home as they root for their teams.

Designed to get people close to the action on the ice, HSBC Arena invites spectators to participate in the game. It's all part of the strong bond Buffalo shares with the multi-purpose HSBC Arena.

Buffalo-Style Chicken Wings

Buffalonians like few things more than watching the Sabres while feasting on a generous helping of Buffalo-Style Chicken Wings. Sabres and Bills fans alike love to enjoy these tasty snacks, which originated in their home city. Use this recipe to fire up your favorite sports fans the next time they sit down to watch the big game.

Prep time: 10 minutes
Cook time: 12 minutes
Yields: 4 servings

24 chicken wings (10 to 12 per pound)

1 cup Frank's Hot Sauce

3/8 cup butter

1/4 teaspoon Worcestershire sauce

1/2 teaspoon garlic powder

1/4 teaspoon onion powder

1/2 tablespoon honey

3 ounces celery sticks

3 ounces carrot sticks

3/4 cup bleu cheese salad dressing

Heat oil in a deep fryer to 350° F.

Place chicken wings in hot oil and fry for 10 to 12 minutes or until browned and cooked through. While the wings are cooking, combine hot sauce, butter, Worcestershire sauce, garlic, onion and honey in a small pan. Warm over medium heat, allowing the butter to melt.

When the wings are done, drain well in a pan lined with paper towels. Place in a large bowl and toss with sauce.

Serve hot with carrot and celery sticks, and bleu cheese dressing on the side.

Lobster
with Butternut Squash Gnocchi

In its native language, gnocchi means "lump." But don't let this recipe's unassuming-sounding side dish fool you. The perfect blend of lobster and butternut squash makes this an offering you can't resist.

Prep time: 30 minutes
Cook time: 60 minutes
Yields: 4 to 6 servings

2 (1 1/2-pound) live Maine lobsters (can use lobster meat if Maine lobsters are unavailable)

Salt

2 tablespoons olive oil plus additional for sautéing

1/2 cup diced onions*

1/2 cup minced leeks, white part only

3/4 cup peeled and diced carrots*

3/4 cup diced celery*

2 peeled and crushed garlic cloves

1 tablespoon tomato paste

1/4 cup cognac or brandy

3 cups fish/seafood stock or water

1 tablespoon finely minced shallots

1 cup heavy cream

1/2 cup grated Fontina cheese

1/2 cup shelled and blanched green peas (can use frozen)

1 tablespoon chopped flat-leaf parsley

1 pound Butternut Squash Gnocchi (see next page)

4 chopped sage leaves

Plunge lobsters headfirst into a pot of boiling, salted water. Cook for 4 minutes. Remove from the water and chill in an ice bath.

Remove the tail and claws from each lobster. Cut the tail in half and crack claws to remove body meat.

Cut meat into 1/2-inch pieces and reserve until needed. Cut body and shells into 2-inch pieces.

Heat olive oil in a skillet over medium-high heat. Add lobster shells and sauté for approximately 4 minutes. Add onions, leeks, carrots, celery and garlic. Sauté for 5 minutes or until onions become translucent.

Add tomato paste to the lobster shells and vegetables. Sauté for 1 minute, stirring constantly. Remove from the burner and add cognac, watching for flame. Add approximately 1 1/2 cups of water or stock and return to stove.

Simmer stock for 20 minutes or until reduced by half. Strain the mixture through a fine strainer, pressing on solids to extract all liquid. Set stock aside.

Heat a medium sauté pan over medium-high heat. Add enough oil to coat the bottom. When hot, add shallots and sauté until translucent.

Add the strained lobster stock and heavy cream. Reduce by half over medium-high heat. Add Fontina cheese and incorporate into cream and stock. Simmer gently until mixture has the consistency of heavy cream.

If sauce is not thick enough (it should coat the back of a spoon), mix 1 teaspoon of cornstarch and 1 tablespoon of cognac. Pour into sauce and cook until the sauce thickens.

Add the lobster pieces and simmer for 5 minutes to allow lobster to finish cooking. Fold in green peas and parsley. Simmer for 1 minute. Season with salt and pepper and reserve warm until needed.

To serve, place a portion of hot gnocchi on a plate. Serve with lobster sauce and finish with chopped sage leaves.

*Dicing should yield 1/4-inch pieces.

Prep time: 40 minutes
Cook time: 15 minutes
Yields: 4 to 6 servings

1 butternut squash, cut in half lengthwise	1/2 teaspoon chopped, fresh sage	White pepper to taste
2 Idaho potatoes	Pinch nutmeg	2 tablespoons butter
1 large egg, beaten	3/4 cup all-purpose flour plus additional flour	1 tablespoon chopped parsley
1/2 cup finely grated Pecorino Romano	to adjust and knead	
1/2 teaspoon chopped, fresh thyme	Kosher salt to taste	

Preheat oven to 375° F.

Arrange squash halves, cut-side down, on a lightly oiled baking sheet. Roast for approximately 40 minutes or until flesh is tender. Remove from oven. When cooled, scoop out the squash flesh, measuring out 3/4 cup. Reserve the rest for another application.

Bake Idaho potatoes for 45 minutes to 1 hour or until flesh is tender. Reserve warm until needed.

Push squash through a mesh sieve or ricer into a large bowl. Add the egg, cheese, herbs, nutmeg and flour. Mix well.

Peel the warm potato and push the flesh through a mesh sieve or ricer into the squash mixture. Mix well and season with salt and pepper.

Wrap the dough tightly and refrigerate for 20 minutes.

Turn dough out onto a floured cutting board and cut into three or four portions. Gently roll each portion into a 3/4-inch-thick log.

Using a floured knife, cut each log into 3/4-inch pieces. Roll the cut pieces of dough into balls.

Using a floured fork, roll the dough out of your palm onto a floured towel.

Cook gnocchi in small batches in boiling salted water for 3 minutes. Transfer from water with slotted spoon to an ice water bath, taking care not to leave them in the water too long. Drain well and reserve until needed.

When ready to serve, heat 2 tablespoons of butter in a large sauté pan. Add gnocchi and cook for 5 to 7 minutes or until golden brown. Finish with fresh, chopped parsley if desired.

"Gnocchi," pronounced "nyo-key," is translated from its native Italian as "dumplings." These are often made with flour, potatoes and eggs, but other versions include spinach, semolina, sweet potatoes, chopped herbs, and Parmesan or ricotta cheese. Once the gnocchi are made, they are cooked in boiling water or broth, and then sauced or tossed with melted butter.

Ralph Wilson Stadium

There are multiple reasons why Ralph Wilson Stadium is near and dear to Buffalonians, and the many Bills fans who live in and around Western New York.

For starters, it has stood as one of the city's icons since it opened its doors in 1973 as Rich Stadium. "The Ralph," as it is known to insiders, hosted the Bills through the glory days of 1990-1993 when the team made four consecutive Super Bowl appearances. And how about January 3, 1993, when the Bills staged the biggest comeback in NFL history by erasing a 35-3 deficit to the Houston Oilers in the second half of the AFC Wild Card Game? The Bills went on to win on a Steve Christie field goal in overtime and eventually advanced to the Super Bowl.

Now equipped with 73,967 seats, 76 dugout suites, 88 club-level boxes and what, at the time of its installation, was one of the first high-definition scoreboards in the NFL, the stadium bears the name of the man who has owned and stood by the ball club since 1959.

Despite Buffalo's reputation for cold and snow, there is no dome on the stadium. Yet, on any given game day, one of every 12 people in the region can be found at the stadium. Rain or shine, as many as 60,000 will be tailgating in the parking lots. The city, the team, the fans are far from afraid of a little adversity.

In the end, the Ralph is just an unbeatable way to spend a Sunday.

Baby Spinach Salad

The beauty of this salad is that you can put just about anything in it. The crisp taste of fresh spinach allows for everything from mandarin oranges to traditional, zesty dressings. Wonderful for chefs who want to indulge their creative sides.

Prep time: 20 minutes
Cook time: 10 minutes
Yields: 4 servings

1 cup olive oil	1 cup medium-diced pancetta	1 (16-ounce) bag stemmed and rinsed baby spinach
1 cup julienned red onions	3/8 cup red wine vinegar	3/4 cup crumbled bleu cheese
Salt to taste	1 tablespoon Dijon mustard	1/2 cup garbanzo beans
Ground black pepper to taste	1 tablespoon sugar	1 pint grape tomatoes

Heat 1/4 cup of olive oil in a medium sauté pan over medium heat. Add red onions, salt and pepper. Sauté until the onions are lightly caramelized by their natural sugar. Cool in refrigerator.

Cook pancetta in sauté pan until crisp. Set aside.

For the dressing, add vinegar, mustard, salt, pepper and sugar to a mixing bowl or a bar blender. With blender on low, slowly add remaining olive oil to vinegar mixture while whisking. Season to taste and add drained pancetta crisps to dressing. Adjust seasoning. Chill.

Place baby spinach in a serving bowl. Arrange chilled red onions in the center of the spinach in an organized fashion. Place bleu cheese around the onions in a full circle. Place rinsed garbanzo beans around the cheese. Gently place tomatoes at outside edge of serving bowl.

Serve dressing on the side in a crock with a ladle.

Traditional Beef on Kimmelweck
with Fresh Horseradish

Bills fans have William Wahr – a German baker – to thank for this regional favorite. Wahr created the dish and brought it to Western New York from Germany's Black Forest. Pretzel salt and caraway seeds cover the top of the roll, while the juicy top round sits within, giving this sandwich a memorable taste.

Prep time: 40 minutes
Cook time: 15 minutes
Yields: 6 servings

FOR THE KIMMELWECK

1/2 tablespoon coarse salt

1/2 tablespoon caraway seeds

1/2 cup cold water

1/2 tablespoon cornstarch

6 Kaiser rolls, parbaked

FOR THE HORSERADISH

1 cup peeled and grated fresh horseradish root

3 tablespoons white vinegar

Kosher salt to taste

1 cup water

For the kimmelweck

Preheat oven to 350° F.

Combine equal parts coarse salt and caraway seeds. Store in a clean jar.

Boil 1/4 cup water in a very small saucepan on the stove or in a small dish in the microwave. Dissolve cornstarch in the remaining 1/4 cup water and add to the boiled water. Place in refrigerator.

Place Kaiser rolls on a baking sheet. Brush the top of the rolls with the cornstarch solution and sprinkle with seed mixture.

Bake for 4 minutes or until seed mixture dries.

For the horseradish

Combine all ingredients. Store in an airtight container until ready to use.

To prepare the sandwich

Heat jus in a small saucepan over medium-high heat until simmering.

Slice kimmelweck rolls horizontally for sandwiches.

Dip approximately 4 ounces (or 1/2 cup) of sliced roast beef in hot jus and place on bottom of roll. Top with a dollop of fresh horseradish and place the top of the kimmelweck over the horseradish.

Note: German potato salad and a dill wedge are perfect accompaniments to Traditional Beef on Kimmelweck.

Hailing from the same family as mustard and cabbage, horseradish is a 3,000-year-old plant whose uses have ranged from a treatment for rheumatism and headaches to an aphrodisiac. More modern and practical uses of the 5-foot-tall plant center around the pungent taste of its large, white root.

Queen City Pot Roast

When the leaves begin to change, Buffalonians look for dishes like this one that bears the nickname of their hometown. Roasting the meat is a daylong process and the aroma is almost as good as the dish itself.

Prep time: 30 minutes
Cook time: 3 hours, 20 minutes
Yields: 12 servings

1 (3- to 4-pound) chuck roast	Kosher salt to taste	1 small peeled and diced rutabaga*
1/4 cup plus 3 tablespoons all-purpose flour	Black pepper to taste	1 medium-diced onion*
1/2 tablespoon onion powder	1 tablespoon olive oil	3 1/4 cups beef broth
1 sprig fresh thyme	5 large peeled and quartered potatoes	1/2 cup red wine
1 tablespoon garlic powder	1 cup baby carrots	

Preheat oven to 275° F.

In a large mixing bowl, toss 1/4 cup flour, onion powder, thyme, garlic powder, salt and black pepper with pot roast.

Heat olive oil over medium-high heat in a roasting pan or deep, covered skillet. Add pot roast and brown on all sides. Add vegetables to brown with pot roast. Remove browned vegetables and set aside.

Add 3 cups of beef broth and all of the red wine to the pot roast and bring to a simmer. (Remaining 1/4 cup of beef broth will be used to thicken the gravy.)

Reduce heat to low and cover the pan. Simmer for 2 1/2 hours. Check doneness with a bamboo skewer after 2 hours, as some cuts may be tender and fully cooked earlier than others.

Remove cover. Add vegetables and any liquid that is with them. Cover again and simmer, checking to see if vegetables are tender after 30 minutes. If not, continue to simmer.

Strain juices into saucepan and bring to a boil. Reduce to a simmer.

Combine remaining 3 tablespoons flour with 1/4 cup of cold beef broth and whisk until smooth. Stir into simmering broth, a little at a time, until desired thickness is achieved. Check seasoning and adjust as needed. Let pot roast rest before slicing.

Arrange sliced pot roast and vegetables on a platter. Drizzle some gravy over the sliced beef and serve gravy on the side.

Dicing should yield 1 1/2 cups medium-diced pieces.

Pastrami Panini

This meaty sandwich draws its name from the type of grill it is cooked on. An ideal combination of melted cheese and meat always has Bills fans coming back for more.

Prep time: 10 minutes
Cook time: 6 minutes
Yields: 3 servings

1 thinly sliced medium, ripe tomato	1 cup shredded cheddar cheese
3 steak rolls of choice	15 ounces sliced deli pastrami
1/4 cup wasabi mayonnaise*	1 1/2 cups julienned green leaf lettuce

Preheat panini grill to 385° F.

Cut steak rolls in half. Spread 2 tablespoons of wasabi mayonnaise on each half of roll. Layer on one half of the roll 1/3 cup of cheese, tomato slices, 5 ounces of pastrami and 1/2 cup of lettuce. Top with the other half of the roll, mayonnaise side down.

Coat panini grill or pan with nonstick cooking spray. Place sandwiches on hot surface and press down firmly on the sandwich with the grill cover or a flat lid. Cook for 6 minutes, occasionally pressing panini.

Slice on the bias and serve warm with chips.

*Mix wasabi powder with just enough water to form a paste. Whisk into mayonnaise to taste.

CHICAGO

Soldier Field

Like every fabled place, Chicago's Soldier Field has a story to tell.

But where to begin? Built in 1924, it is the granddaddy of the NFL venues...a downtown stadium that has been the official home of the Chicago Bears for decades.

It is a venerable old place. True, a 2003 rebuild did much to bring the stadium up to modern-day standards. But it didn't chase away the ghosts of the likes of George Halas, Gale Sayers and Brian Piccolo, Mike Ditka, Walter Payton and all of the Monsters of the Midway. And for that, Bears fans surely must be grateful.

The memories of the 1926 Army vs. Navy college football game during which the stadium was officially dedicated and the "The Long Count," a 1927 official heavyweight bout between Jack Dempsey and Gene Tunney, are alive and well. But so are more recent events such as the opening ceremonies for the 1994 World Cup, the 2005 Rolling Stones performance and other concerts that serve as a listing of who's who in music history.

Architectural details like the iconic columns at the main gate have been preserved. So, too, the stadium continues to stand as a symbol of freedom, a memorial to American soldiers who sacrificed their lives. The stadium's grounds still feature benches embedded with medals and relief images of leaves to represent fallen soldiers.

All of this ensures that when visitors to the field come to hear the sounds and sights of sports and music, they're also immersed in the sounds and the sights of America.

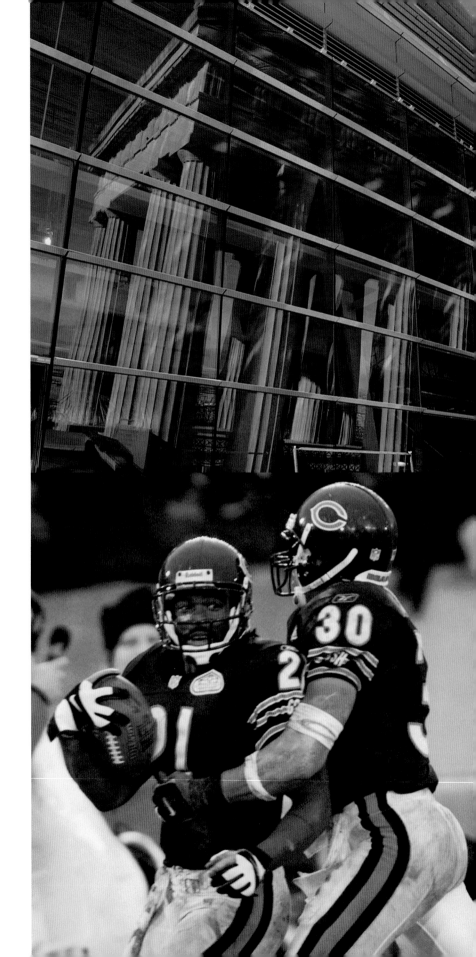

Sun-Dried Tomato Onion Dip

This recipe is a new take on the ever-popular French onion soup. Try pairing it with pita points or tortilla chips for a dip your guests will not soon forget.

Prep time: 12 minutes
Cook time: 15 minutes plus 40 minutes for roasting onion
Yields: 3 cups

1 medium, peeled Spanish onion	1/2 cup water	2 cups sour cream
2 tablespoons canola oil	1 tablespoon French onion soup mix	5/8 cup mayonnaise
1 clove garlic	1 tablespoon red wine vinegar	Kosher salt to taste
2 sprigs fresh thyme	2 tablespoons sun-dried tomatoes	Ground black pepper to taste

Preheat oven to 335° F.

Toss half of the onion in oil, garlic and thyme. Wrap in foil and roast for 40 to 50 minutes or until onion is golden brown. Reserve the other half of the onion for another use. When onion is done, remove and chill.

Pour half of the water (i.e., 1/4 cup) into a small microwave-safe bowl. Microwave on high until water begins to boil. Remove from microwave oven and add soup mix. Let stand for 10 minutes to rehydrate.

In another small microwave-safe bowl, boil red wine vinegar and the other half of the water. Remove from microwave oven. Add sun-dried tomatoes and let rehydrate for 10 minutes.

Remove thyme sprig from roasted onion mixture.

Using a food processor, purée sun-dried tomato mixture with roasted onion and garlic. Add remaining ingredients and mix well. Check seasonings and adjust as needed.

Serve with kettle-style potato chips.

Spinach and Artichoke Dip

Keep it simple and at the same time, show off your culinary skills with this timeless recipe. With so many different cheeses and spices mixed in, this dip can stand alone or be paired with numerous other dishes.

Prep time: 25 minutes
Cook time: 20 minutes
Yields: 5 (1-cup) servings

1 pound frozen, chopped spinach	1 1/4 cups loose, shredded Swiss cheese	12 ounces roughly chopped canned artichoke hearts
3 cups shredded Asiago cheese	1 1/4 cups shredded Jarlsberg cheese	1/4 cup bock beer (or your favorite beer)
1 cup mayonnaise	1 tablespoon finely chopped garlic	Kosher salt to taste
1/2 cup heavy cream	3 tablespoons thinly sliced scallions	Ground black pepper to taste
1/2 cup sour cream	1 tablespoon chopped parsley	

Preheat oven to 350° F.

Place spinach in a bowl. Squeeze dry.

Separate 1/2 cup Asiago cheese and retain for garnish.

In a large bowl, add spinach, mayonnaise, heavy cream, sour cream and cheeses and combine well. Add garlic, scallions, parsley and artichokes. Mix briefly to incorporate. Slowly add beer while scraping the sides of the bowl.

Fill a 2-quart ovenproof casserole or au gratin dish three-quarters full and top with remaining Asiago cheese.

Bake uncovered for 35 minutes or until dip is bubbling hot and cheese on top is light brown.

Serve accompanied by toasted baguette slices.

Few foods are healthier than spinach, which is chock-full of vitamins A, C, E and K, along with iron, magnesium and several other antioxidants. Spinach is believed to have originated more than a millennium ago in southeastern Asia, spreading to Europe, where the ancient Greek and Roman empires cultivated it. European settlers eventually brought it with them to the New World.

Monster of the Midway Chili

This famous chili has been keeping Bears fans toasty at Soldier Field for decades. Now it can keep guests in your home warm while they watch their favorite team. Combine with Spanish Rice or Salsa Fresca for even more flavor.

Prep time: 20 minutes
Cook time: 50 minutes
Yields: 4 (1-cup) servings

1 pound 80/20 ground beef*

2 tablespoons minced garlic

1/4 cup diced Spanish onion**

2 chipotle chilies from a can, in adobo,
   finely chopped

2 tablespoons ground cumin

3 tablespoons chili powder

2 tablespoons masa harina (corn flour)

1 cup canned tomato sauce

1 cup canned chili sauce

1 cup canned, diced tomatoes

1 cup drained and rinsed canned kidney beans

1 cup rinsed and drained canned
   Great Northern beans

1 cup beef stock

1/2 teaspoon dried oregano

Kosher salt to taste

Freshly ground black pepper to taste

Place ground beef in a 3- to 4-quart heavy-bottom saucepan preheated over medium-high heat. When beef is browned, add garlic, onions, cumin, chopped chilies and chili powder. Sauté over medium heat for 3 minutes or until onions are translucent.

Add masa harina and combine well. Add remaining ingredients and simmer approximately 30 minutes or until liquid has thickened.

Taste and adjust seasoning with salt and pepper.

Serve in a bowl. Garnish with shredded cheddar cheese, diced onions, sour cream and tortilla chips.

*Meat cutters routinely use this designation to indicate the approximate ratio of lean meat to fat.
**Dicing should yield 1/4-inch pieces.

U.S. Cellular Field

When Gene Cernan became the last man to leave his footprints on the moon in 1972, he mused about his friend Neil Armstrong who upstaged him three years earlier by being the first. "What do you say after Neil? Who is ever going to remember anything other than, 'That's one small step for man?'"

The builders of what is now Chicago's U.S. Cellular Field might well have had a similar worry: Who's ever going to remember anything other than the original Comiskey Park?

The grand old house of the White Sox for 80 years was hallowed, to be sure. However, in the almost-20 years since New Comiskey Park opened its gates, it has proven itself a worthy successor. The ballpark that is now U.S. Cellular Field can hold over 44,000 people, and contains more than 80 luxury boxes and numerous dining options to give White Sox fans everything they want.

Including a fifth World Series title and an end to a dry spell – one of the longest in the majors – that began in 1917. Keyed by talent such as Jermaine Dye and Paul Konerko, the White Sox swept the Houston Astros in 2005 to earn the title.

The White Sox franchise is brimming with history. With roots going back to 1893, the South Siders demonstrated early on what the best and worst of sports – and humanity – are all about. After all, it was eight Sox who were accused of fixing the 1919 World Series. And when the judge in the infamous Black Sox trial banned them from playing professional baseball for life after their acquittal, team owner Charles Comiskey supported Landis's decision even though it essentially destroyed his top-ranked team.

But that's in the past. One of the oldest franchises in baseball has retired the numbers of such greats as Nellie Fox, Harold Baines and Carlton Fisk, each spring bringing the promise of America's greatest pastime to the South Side of Chicago.

Salsa Fresca

There is salsa, and then there is fresh salsa. Those hoping to understand the difference should take the time to create this recipe.

Prep time: 15 minutes
Cook time: 15 to 20 minutes
Yields: 4 cups

8 washed and cored Roma tomatoes

1 1/4 peeled, large red onions

1 bunch scallions

2 tablespoons olive oil

Salt to taste

Ground black pepper to taste

1 1/2 tablespoons canned chipotle in adobo purée

Juice from 4 limes

1 tablespoon ground cumin

1 tablespoon chili powder

2 cups tomato juice

3/4 cup chopped cilantro

1/4 cup chopped parsley

Preheat grill to a medium-high temperature.

Prepare fresh vegetables by cutting tomatoes in half lengthwise, cutting onions in 1/4-inch rounds and trimming the ends off the scallions. Toss the vegetables in separate bowls with olive oil, salt and pepper.

Grill vegetables until done, but not overcooked. Cool. Slice the scallions, and dice the tomatoes and onions into small pieces.

Combine the vegetables with the remaining ingredients and place in the refrigerator overnight or no less than 2 hours.

Serve with your favorite chips.

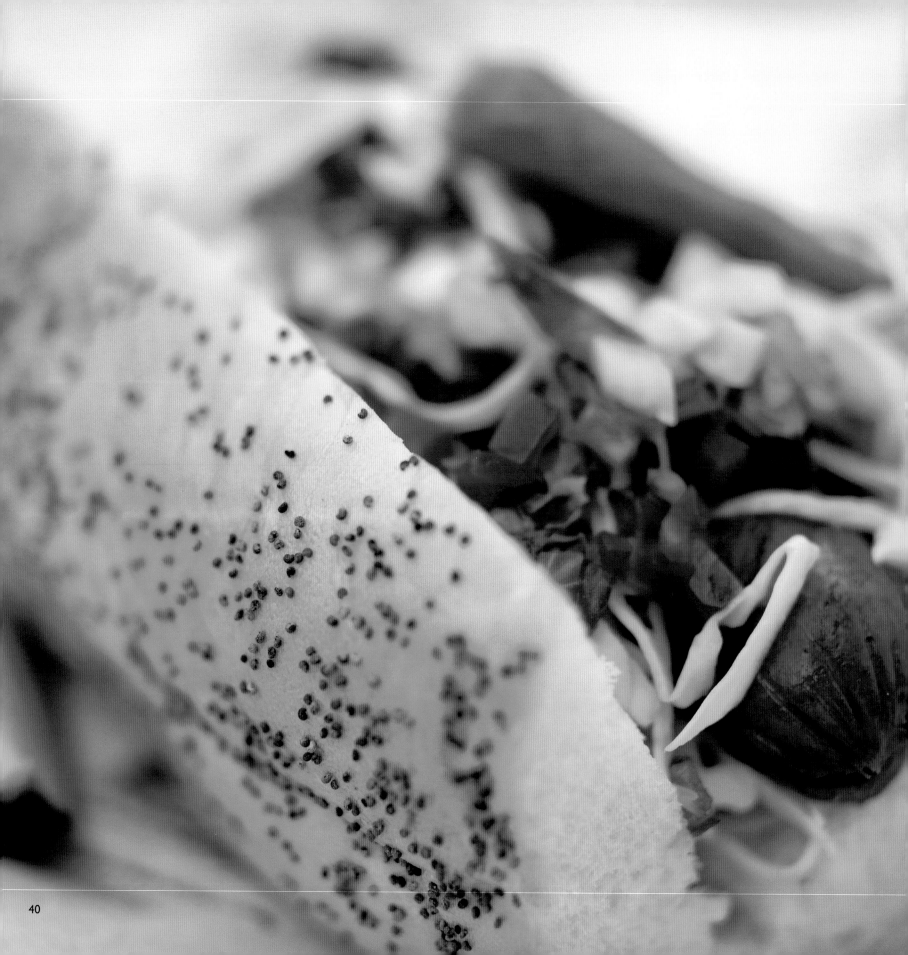

Chicago Hot Dog

Every city loves to put its own twist on the hot dog, and Chicago is no different. Equipped with neon relish, sport peppers, diced tomatoes and a poppy seed bun, the Chicago Hot Dog is a year-round treat.

Prep time: 5 minutes
Cook time: 5 minutes
Yields: 1 serving

1 (4-ounce) natural-casing, all-beef hot dog	2 tablespoons neon pickle relish	1 crisp kosher pickle spear
1 poppy seed bun	2 tablespoons diced onions	3 sport peppers
1 tablespoon yellow mustard	2 tomato wedges	Celery salt to taste

Steam hot dog until internal temperature is above 170° F. (Hot dog can also be boiled, but steaming is preferable.)

Steam a poppy seed bun until soft, but not soggy. Place hot dog in steamed poppy seed bun.

Top with yellow mustard, neon relish, diced onions, tomato, pickle spear and sport peppers. Finish with a dash of celery salt.

When and how the Chicago-style hot dog came about is a matter of debate. But the record reflects that it was served in 1893 at the Chicago World's Fair. So for more than a century, Chicagoans have been eating and crowing about one of their tastiest claims to fame.

You can barely turn around in the Windy City without bumping into a hot dog joint. Every local seemingly has a favorite spot, not to mention a definite idea about the variations that are acceptable and the ones that fall more naturally into the category of blasphemy. Our chefs insist the relish should be bright, neon green; the mustard, yellow. Most importantly, ketchup should never touch a Chicago dog. If you must have it, put it on your French fries.

CINCINNATI

Great American Ball Park

The opening of a baseball stadium is generally regarded as a big day in the life of a city. But when it manages to capture the nation's attention, it's something else.

The inauguration of Cincinnati's Great American Ball Park took place March 31, 2003. Fans who came for opening day found American flags waiting for them at their seats. And with the United States newly at war with Iraq, the crowd saw seemingly every event of the Reds' opener as a reason to wave the star-spangled banners.

The team presented a bald eagle to the Cincinnati Zoo just moments before the game. Then, the 41st president of the United States, George W. Bush, took the field to throw out the first pitch. Following the national anthem, red, white and blue streamers shot into the stands and fans couldn't help but chant, "U-S-A."

The Reds lost their first game at Great American Ball Park, but the stadium has continued to live up to its opening-day hype. State-of-the-art design, coupled with culinary draws like the Riverside Club, gives fans the chance to experience more than just a baseball game when they visit the park. Statues of past Reds greats like Frank Robinson and Ernie Lombardi pay tribute to legendary ballplayers who've worn the Reds jersey.

Crispy Mozzarella Medallions

Take the time to use hickory wood chips for this recipe and you'll discover a unique, smoky flavor. Sweet tomato chutney complements the medallions with a hint of sweetness.

Prep time: 1 hour
Cook time: 1 hour
Yields: 24 (1/2-inch) servings

10 seeded and coarsely chopped, ripe Roma tomatoes	Salt to taste	24 pieces thinly sliced Prosciutto de Parma
1 cup finely diced red onion	Ground black pepper to taste	2 cups all-purpose flour
2 teaspoons finely minced garlic	1 tablespoon dried oregano	4 large eggs, beaten with 3 tablespoons water
1 cup red wine vinegar	1 tablespoon dried thyme	4 cups seasoned breadcrumbs
3/4 cup brown sugar	2 pounds Buffalo mozzarella (can use regular mozzarella)	2 cups shredded green cabbage
1 (8-ounce) can tomato paste	1 quart canola oil	1 cup thinly sliced fennel bulb
		1/3 cup Italian salad dressing

Prepare tomato chutney by combining the Roma tomatoes, red onion, garlic, red wine vinegar, brown sugar, tomato paste, salt, pepper, oregano and thyme in a medium saucepan. Cook over medium-low heat for 25 minutes. Reserve and keep warm.

Cut mozzarella into 1/2-inch slices.

Pour the oil into a deep fryer or large cast-iron skillet. Heat oil to 350° F.

Carefully wrap each slice of mozzarella with a thin strip of prosciutto. Dredge the medallions in the flour, followed by the egg mixture and the seasoned breadcrumbs.

Place the medallions back in the egg mixture and then again in the breadcrumbs. Refrigerate until ready to fry.

To prepare the Italian slaw, place the shredded cabbage in a bowl with the fennel and Italian dressing. Toss well. Refrigerate until needed.

Carefully drop the medallions into the hot oil and fry approximately 3 minutes or until light golden brown.

Remove the mozzarella medallions and place on paper towels to absorb excess oil.

To serve, place the Italian slaw in the center of a serving tray. Lay the medallions around the slaw mixture and top with the tomato chutney.

Serve warm.

Mozzarella gets its name from the Italian verb "mozzare," which means to cut, a reference to the cutting and spinning involved in its creation. Fresh mozzarella – the choice of virtually all chefs – contains no preservatives and is usually served on the day it is made. The difference in taste, they maintain, is indisputable.

Cincinnati Chili

This regional take on chili is usually served as a topping sauce or over spaghetti. According to the Greater Cincinnati Convention and Visitors Bureau, more than 2 million pounds of the famous mixture are eaten each year by Ohio sports fans.

Prep time: 20 minutes
Cook time: 45 minutes
Yields: 8 servings

1 chopped, large red onion	1 teaspoon ground cumin	1 (15-ounce) can tomato sauce
1 pound 80/20 ground beef	1/2 teaspoon red (cayenne) pepper	1 tablespoon Worcestershire sauce
1 minced garlic clove	1/2 teaspoon salt	1 tablespoon red wine vinegar
1 tablespoon chili powder	1 teaspoon ground black pepper	
1 teaspoon ground cinnamon	1/2 cup melted semi-sweet chocolate	

In a large frying pan over medium heat, sauté onion, ground beef, garlic and chili powder until ground beef is slightly cooked. Add the rest of the ingredients. Reduce heat to low and simmer, uncovered, for 45 minutes. Remove from heat.

Note: Chili can be served as a topping for hot dogs or simply enjoyed by itself.

Bleu Cheese and Fig Salad

Crumbly bleu cheese covers this traditional fig salad to create a great dish to serve alongside an entrée. Guests will enjoy this recipe, which steps away from the common salad.

Prep time: 20 minutes
Yields: 2 to 4 servings

1 to 2 cups unpeeled, julienned Asian pears

1 tablespoon apple cider vinegar

3 cups gourmet spring salad mix

1/4 cup maytag bleu cheese

1 cup dried and quartered figs

1 1/2 cups Pomegranate Vinaigrette (see below)

2 tablespoons lime or lemon juice

Toss pears with vinegar to prevent them from discoloring.

Wash and dry lettuce and place in a bowl. Top with the bleu cheese crumbles and figs.

Drizzle the dressing over the lettuce, figs and bleu cheese. Finish with julienne pears. Add 2 tablespoons of lime or lemon juice for acidity.

Pomegranate Vinaigrette

Prep time: 10 minutes
Cook time: 15 minutes
Yields: 2 cups

1 cup pomegranate juice

1 minced, medium shallot

1/2 cup champagne vinegar

1 cup extra-virgin olive oil

Salt to taste

Ground black pepper to taste

Place pomegranate juice in a small saucepan over medium heat. Simmer for 15 minutes or until juice is reduced by half. Remove from heat and set aside to cool.

Combine shallots, vinegar and pomegranate juice. Purée in a bar blender. While the blender is on medium speed, slowly pour in the olive oil. Adjust seasonings to taste.

Great American Stuffed Pork Loin
with Spicy Tomato Cream Sauce

In the heart of what has long been nicknamed Porkopolis, Great American Ball Park chefs use this recipe to put their own spin on traditional pork. This is a high-end dish that is well worth the preparation time.

Prep time: 20 minutes
Cook time: 40 minutes
Yields: 6 to 8 servings

1/4 pound diced pancetta*

1/4 cup chopped Spanish onion

2 teaspoons chopped garlic

1/2 teaspoon chopped thyme

1 tablespoon unsalted butter

6 ounces washed baby spinach

1/8 cup toasted pine nuts**

1/4 pound crumbled gorgonzola cheese

1 cup unseasoned breadcrumbs

Kosher salt to taste

Ground black pepper to taste

1 (4-pound) center-cut pork loin

Vegetable oil

2 cups Spicy Tomato Cream Sauce (see page 49)

Preheat oven to 350° F.

Heat a medium sauté pan over medium-high heat. Add pancetta and onions and cook together until the onions are soft and pancetta is crisp.

Add garlic, thyme, butter and spinach. Lightly sauté the spinach until it's wilted. Set aside and let cool completely.

Once the spinach mixture is cool, add the pine nuts, the gorgonzola cheese and the breadcrumbs, and mix well. Taste and season with salt and pepper, if desired.

Make a 1-inch cut down the entire pork loin and fill with the spinach mixture. Use butcher's twine to tie the ends of the pork loin. Season outside with salt and pepper.

Heat a large sauté pan over medium-high heat. Add enough oil to coat the bottom. Sear the pork loin in the hot oil, turning until all sides are golden brown. Transfer pork to a roasting pan with a rack. Roast in preheated oven for 35 minutes or until internal temperature reaches 155° F.

Remove from the oven and let rest at least 10 minutes. Remove butcher's twine and slice roast. Serve hot with Spicy Tomato Cream Sauce.

*Dicing should yield 1/4-inch pieces.

**To toast pine nuts, preheat oven to 350° F. Place nuts in a shallow baking dish and roast for 5 minutes or until golden brown. Let cool.

Prep time: 15 minutes
Cook time: 80 minutes
Yields: 2 cups

2 tablespoons olive oil

1 peeled and roughly chopped, medium carrot

1/2 peeled and chopped, medium Spanish onion

1 finely chopped stalk celery

2 (12-ounce) cans diced tomatoes

2 cups chicken broth

1 tablespoon crushed red pepper flakes

1 large pinch thyme leaves

1 large pinch oregano

1 tablespoon tomato paste

2 cups heavy whipping cream

Kosher salt to taste

Black pepper to taste

Heat oil in the bottom of a medium saucepan. Sauté onions, celery and carrots over medium heat for 10 minutes or until onions are translucent.

Combine all ingredients except heavy cream. Bring to a slow boil and cook for 1 hour or until sauce mixture thickens, stirring often to avoid scorching the bottom of the sauce.

Remove saucepan from the heat. Transfer sauce to a blender and purée.* Transfer puréed sauce mixture back to the saucepan and add the heavy whipping cream. Cook for 10 minutes longer or until cream thickens. Season with salt and pepper to taste.

When blending something hot, cover the lid with a towel so the liquid won't splash out.

Fried Cookie Dough

It's not unusual to see Cincinnati Reds fans walking through the ballpark sampling Fried Cookie Dough from the paper bags it is served in. Unique to Great American Ball Park, this recipe is quick and sinfully delicious.

Prep time: 10 minutes
Cook time: 10 minutes
Yields: 20 tablespoon-size balls

FOR THE DOUGH

1 1/8 cups all-purpose flour

1/2 teaspoon baking soda

1/2 teaspoon salt

1/2 cup softened butter

1/3 cup plus 1 teaspoon granulated sugar

1/3 cup brown sugar

1/2 teaspoon vanilla extract

1 large egg

1 cup semi-sweet chocolate chips

FOR THE BATTER

2 cups funnel cake batter mix or regular
  waffle batter mix

1 1/5 cups water

1/4 cup powdered sugar

1 cup chocolate sauce

1 cup whipped cream

For the dough

Mix flour, baking soda, salt, butter, granulated sugar and brown sugar with an electric mixer until fully combined. Add vanilla and egg, and mix well. Fold in the chocolate chips and mix until just combined.

Using floured hands, divide the dough into 20 uniform tablespoon-size balls. Freeze.

For the batter

Using a deep fryer, preheat 1 quart of vegetable oil to 375° F.

Mix the funnel cake batter and water in a large bowl. Using a fork, coat frozen dough balls by dipping them into the batter. Carefully drop one at a time into the hot oil, gently shaking the basket to make sure the dough doesn't stick to the bottom. Fry approximately 3 to 4 minutes or until dough is golden brown.

Remove dough from oil and place in a dish lined with paper towels. To serve, sprinkle the fried cookie dough with powdered sugar and place on a plate striped with chocolate sauce. Serve with a side of whipped cream for dipping.

CLEVELAND

Cleveland Browns Stadium

Ask any seasoned NFL fan about Cleveland Browns Stadium, and it will be only a matter of time before the infamous Dawg Pound comes to light.

The bleacher section behind the east end zone in the stadium is famous for its collection of 10,644 of some of the most fun-loving — albeit rabid — spectators in the NFL. Named after the 1985 defensive line cornerback Hanford Dixon dubbed "the dawgs," members of the pound have been known to don canine masks and hurl dog biscuits to express their displeasure.

But that's just part of the Cleveland story. The stadium was built in 1999 on the same footprint as its predecessor, Cleveland Municipal Stadium. The Browns' new home is a true 21st-century facility with numerous modern amenities. The venue holds 73,200 football fans and boasts 134 luxury suites.

It's a worthy home for a team with a storied past and what looks to be a bright future. The team has had the fortune of retiring the numbers of such football legends as Jim Brown and Otto Graham. Recently, the Browns organization put together one of its more successful drafts by snaring both offensive lineman Joe Thomas and quarterback Brady Quinn in the first round.

That's good news for loyal members of the Dawg Pound. Fully aware they exist in a great stadium capable of speaking for itself, they still feel obligated to make sure Browns opponents hear them loudly and clearly.

Lettuce Wraps

One of the newer culinary trends in the world, lettuce wraps work equally well as appetizers as they do entrées. A substitute for tortillas and pitas, the lettuce wraps are healthy and full of taste.

Prep time: 35 minutes
Cook time: 10 minutes
Yields: 4 to 6 servings

2 cups soft Asian chow mein noodles

1/4 cup sesame oil

3/4 pound uncooked julienned chicken breast*

Salt to taste

Ground black pepper to taste

1 cup sweet chili sauce

1 cup hoisin sauce

1/2 cup finely julienned red onions

1/2 cup finely julienned red peppers

1/2 cup finely julienned zucchinis

1/2 cup finely julienned carrots

1 large head cored Boston bib lettuce
 (leave whole on a plate)

Drop noodles into boiling salted water and cook for 3 minutes or until tender. Drain.

Pour 2 tablespoons of sesame oil over noodles. Toss and let cool. Refrigerate until needed.

Heat additional sesame oil in a medium skillet over medium-high heat. Sauté chicken until golden brown and fully cooked, adding salt and pepper to taste. Set aside and place in refrigerator.

Arrange vegetables (except lettuce) on a large service platter, placing a 1-cup ramekin of sweet chili sauce at one end and a 1-cup ramekin of hoisin sauce at the other. Place noodles and chicken breast strips in separate serving bowls and place to the side of the platter.

To serve, take one lettuce cup or leaf, add chicken, noodles and choice of vegetables.

Top with your choice of sauce.

Chicken pieces should be 1/4 inch by 1/4 inch by 1/2 inch.

Olive Tapenade

Popular in the south of France, tapenade consists of puréed or finely chopped black olives that form the basis of a paste that works as well as an hors d'oeuvre spread as it does as a filling for meat and fish. A variety of herbs, spices and other ingredients can be used to vary the recipe.

Prep time: 15 minutes
Cook time: None
Yields: 2 cups

1 cup ripe olives

1 cup green olives

1 1/2 teaspoons fresh garlic

1/4 cup peeled and chopped carrot

1 tablespoon chopped onion

1 tablespoon chopped, fresh parsley

1 tablespoon olive oil

Salt to taste

Ground black pepper to taste

Combine all ingredients except olive oil, salt and pepper in a food processor. Using the pulse feature, chop all ingredients until pieces are somewhat uniform in size. Slowly pour olive oil in mixture and continue chopping. Season with salt and pepper to taste.

Progressive Field

Those who get a chance to visit downtown Cleveland and take in a game at Progressive Field may quickly decide this is a stadium defined by the city within which it resides. That's good news for Progressive Field, considering the rich history, architecture and culture that abound in downtown Cleveland.

Recognizing this, when Indians owners Richard and David Jacobs commissioned the building of Jacobs Field in 1992, they made sure the stadium would blend in with its surroundings. From its exposed steel design, which looks similar to so many bridges on the North coast, to the vertical light towers that match smokestacks found in Cleveland's industrial areas, the ballpark that is now called Progressive Field is truly a mirror of the city.

It is likewise a monument to 130 years of Cleveland baseball, illustrating a point: The city and the sport are blood brothers.

On top of picturesque views of downtown and Lake Erie, Progressive Field boasts some of the plushest seats in the majors. The park has more legroom and wider aisles than most stadiums; better elevation between rows gives way to clear and unobstructed views.

Cleveland has virtually all the attributes of a Midwestern city, including winters that can be harsh. But when it's summer and the sun is still high over the lake, all anyone can think about is, "Play ball."

55

Cleveland Bomber

Cleveland's famous roast beef tortilla may play off of the Philadelphia Cheese Steak Sandwich, but it has its own rich flavor. Marinated roast beef combines with melted cheese and a crisp tortilla shell to create a sandwich that oozes flavor.

Prep time: 10 minutes
Cook time: 5 minutes
Yields: 4 sandwiches

1 1/2 pounds shaved top round roast beef

1 1/4 cups beef broth

1/2 cup chopped spicy giardiniera peppers

4 (16-inch) flour tortillas

1/2 cup shredded mozzarella cheese

Cook roast beef and broth in a medium saucepan until beef is well done. Drain beef and reserve liquid.

On the center of each flour tortilla, place 6 ounces of the drained beef, 2 tablespoons of giardiniera peppers and 2 tablespoons of shredded mozzarella cheese.

Roll the tortilla like a burrito. Serve au jus and with potato chips or French fries.

Honey-Glazed Duck Breast
with Baby Greens and Cranberry Apricot Compote

A perfect recipe for summertime. The numerous citrus flavors are refreshing during hot days and warm nights. What has become a fan favorite at Progressive Field can now be replicated at home. It's a perfect dining option after watching a big Indians win.

Prep time: 20 minutes
Cook time: 8 to 10 minutes (medium-rare)
Yields: 4 servings

4 (6-ounce) duck breasts

1 tablespoon honey

4 servings Baby Greens (see below)

1 cup Cranberry Apricot Compote (see below)

Preheat oven to 350° F.

Score skin of duck breast with a sharp knife. Place meat skin side down in a large, preheated sauté pan. Cook over low heat for 12 to 15 minutes or until skin is crisp. Turn meat over.

Brush with honey and bake approximately 8 to 10 minutes or until the internal temperature reaches 125° F for medium-rare. Allow the duck breast to rest for 10 minutes before slicing.

To serve, place one-quarter of the Baby Greens on each plate. Add the sliced duck breast and garnish with Cranberry Apricot Compote.

Note: Add an apple slice and cheese wedges for garnish.

Baby Greens

Prep time: 8 minutes
Yields: 4 servings

1 medium zested and juiced lemon

1/2 cup extra-virgin olive oil

Kosher salt to taste

Ground black pepper to taste

16 ounces baby field greens

Combine the lemon juice and olive oil in a bowl. Add zest and season with kosher salt and ground black pepper to taste.

Place baby field greens in a large bowl and toss with dressing.

Cranberry Apricot Compote

Prep time: 2 minutes
Cook time: 8 minutes
Yields: 1 cup

1/2 cup sliced, dried apricots

1/2 cup white wine

3/4 cup cranberry sauce

2 tablespoons granulated sugar

Place apricots in a small skillet over medium heat. Add white wine and cook for 3 to 5 minutes or until white wine is reduced by half.

Stir in cranberry sauce and sugar. Cook mixture for 2 to 3 minutes, stirring occasionally until compote thickens.

Remove from heat, cool and reserve until needed.

Lake Erie Walleye
with Anna Potatoes, Roasted Corn Relish and Spicy Tartar Sauce

---

Fishermen who get fresh walleye out of Lake Erie distribute them to local venues, and Progressive Field never misses out. Take advantage of this delicious fish in your own home with this recipe.

Prep time: 20 minutes
Cook time: 4 minutes
Yields: 4 servings

2 quarts vegetable oil

4 (8-ounce) skinned and boned walleye filets

2 tablespoons seasoned salt

2 large eggs

1/2 cup all-purpose flour

1/2 cup Panko breadcrumbs

Heat oil in a deep fryer or large cast-iron skillet to 325° F.

Cut each walleye filet into three pieces and add seasoned salt.

Create a breading station by whipping eggs in a large bowl, placing flour in another large bowl with seasoned salt, and placing breadcrumbs in a third large bowl.

Dredge walleye in flour, shaking off excess. Place on a flat pan.

Then dredge in egg and repeat in breadcrumbs. The filet should be well coated.

Place breaded walleye filets into the deep fryer and cook for 3 to 4 minutes or until golden brown.

Set filets on a plate lined with paper towels to absorb excess oil.

Lake Erie, which was in large part responsible for Cleveland's standing as a twentieth-century industrial power, also gives it one of its favorite sports and tastiest menu items. Walleye fill the Great Lake by the tens of millions, occupying every area of it and some of its major tributaries as well.

Anna Potatoes

Prep time: 10 minutes
Cook time: 35 to 40 minutes
Yields: 6 servings

5 large Yukon Gold potatoes
1/4 cup vegetable oil
Kosher salt to taste

Ground black pepper to taste
1/2 cup butter

Preheat oven to 300° F.

Thinly slice potatoes using a mandolin or V-slicer. Coat slices with some of the vegetable oil to prevent them from discoloring.

Season potatoes with salt and pepper.

Heat small (8- or 9-inch) nonstick skillet over medium heat. Add 1 tablespoon of oil.

Add sliced potatoes to hot skillet, one slice at a time, overlapping in a circle for three complete rotations (approximately 1/2 to 3/4 inch thick). Add butter to each of the layers.

Allow potatoes to cook over medium heat for 4 to 5 minutes or until edges turn golden brown. Flip potatoes with spatula and cook for another 3 to 5 minutes.

Place in oven for 30 to 35 minutes. Remove from oven and pour off excess oil/butter.

Slide potatoes onto cutting board. Cut into wedges before plating.

Roasted Corn Relish

Prep time: 10 to 12 minutes
Cook time: 8 minutes
Yields: 2 cups

3/4 cup whole kernel corn
3/8 cup diced green bell peppers
3/8 cup diced red bell peppers

3/8 cup diced red onions
3 tablespoons olive oil

Kosher salt to taste
Ground black pepper to taste

Preheat oven to 350° F.

Place corn, peppers and onions in a bowl. Toss with olive oil and season with salt and pepper.

Place mixture in a small (8- or 9-inch) nonstick sauté pan. Place in oven for 7 to 8 minutes or until mixture is soft and starting to brown, stirring once or twice during baking.

Remove from oven and allow to cool.

Spicy Tartar Sauce

Prep time: 5 minutes
Yields: 2 cups

1 1/4 cups mayonnaise	1 tablespoon Dijon mustard	Salt to taste
1/2 cup sweet pickle relish	1 1/2 teaspoons Cajun spice	Ground black pepper to taste
3/8 cup finely chopped red onion	2 tablespoons lemon juice	

Combine all ingredients in a bowl and mix well with a spatula. Chill mixture in refrigerator until ready to serve. Add salt and pepper to taste.

Crème Brûlée

Crème brûlée is a French dessert consisting of a rich custard base topped with a layer of hard caramel that is created by caramelizing sugar under intense heat.

Prep time: 8 minutes
Cook time: 1 hour, 20 minutes
Yields: 5 (4-ounce) servings

2 1/2 cups heavy cream	1/2 cup plus 1 tablespoon granulated sugar	6 large strawberries
Paste from 1/2 vanilla bean	3 eggs	24 blueberries
(scrape inside of bean with a spoon)	2 tablespoons brown sugar	

Preheat oven to 300° F. In a heavy-bottom saucepan, heat heavy cream, vanilla bean paste and 1/2 cup sugar over medium heat, stirring occasionally, until a low boil occurs.

In a stainless steel bowl, whisk eggs and 1 tablespoon sugar together.

Temper eggs with one-third of the amount of hot cream mixture. Then add tempered mixture into saucepan and stir.

Cook until mixture is 190° F or thick enough to coat the back of a spoon. Remove from heat and strain.

Pour strained mixture into five single-serving baking dishes or ramekins. Place dishes in a deep baking pan with water bath one-quarter of the way up the sides of the ramekins. Place in oven.

Bake for 1 hour or until custard is almost set (it will be slightly loose in the middle). Remove ramekins from water bath and refrigerate overnight.

When ready to serve, lightly coat tops of ramekins with a dusting of brown sugar and caramelize under broiler until golden brown. Serve crème brûlée with fresh fruit.

COLUMBUS

Nationwide Arena

When *Columbus Dispatch* sportswriter Bob Hunter reported on Nationwide Arena's hosting of the 2007 NHL draft, he was careful to state the obvious: "The city will always be known for football first...." Then Hunter went out on a limb. "...But last night provided further proof that if the Blue Jackets ever win, this place will go nuts."

Adding to Nationwide Arena's reputation for embodying the best a modern hockey venue has to offer players and spectators was the draft. Complete with a packed arena — an oddity for this event — and a party on Front Street that wouldn't stop, the home of the Columbus Blue Jackets put many of the league's brightest stars on the path to fame that night. It also made a point: Hockey in Columbus is a close second to football. Very close.

Built in 2000, Nationwide Arena is an 800,000-square-foot facility that can seat more than 18,000 fans for a hockey game. The facility is unique in the NHL in that it houses the Dispatch Icehaus, a small ice rink used for team practices, youth hockey games and recreational skating for Columbus residents. It is also a frequent stop for first-rate touring musicians and shows.

Will Nationwide ever surpass Ohio Stadium in recognition and popularity? Will hockey in Columbus ever become the religion that college football is? It seems a lot of people are no longer even asking the question.

Meateor Wings

If you're trying to picture a Meateor Wing, think of a chicken wing blown up about five times and full of turkey. Mix and match your favorite sauce with these wings and you'll create something everyone will love.

Prep time: 8 minutes
Cook time: 12 to 15 minutes
Yields: 4 servings

2 tablespoons butter or margarine

1 1/2 cups vinegar-based hot pepper sauce

4 pounds turkey wings

6 ounces bleu cheese salad dressing

3 ounces celery sticks

3 ounces carrot sticks

Heat oil in a deep fryer to 375° F.

Melt butter or margarine in a small saucepan. Mix in hot sauce. Reserve warm until needed.

Place wings in the hot oil and fry for 15 to 17 minutes or until the internal temperature is 160° F and the wings are golden brown. Remove the wings from the oil and drain well on paper towels.

Place wings in a large mixing bowl and pour in sauce to coat.

Serve hot with bleu cheese dressing, and celery and carrot sticks.

German Short Ribs

One of the most popular cuts of beef, short ribs are traditionally larger and meatier than their pork counterpart, baby back ribs. Short ribs enable chefs to be creative; a number of cooking methods can be employed. Here, the ribs are slow cooked in a delightful tomato juice blend for maximum flavor.

Prep time: 15 minutes
Cook time: 3 hours
Yields: 4 servings

1 1/2 cups tomato juice	1 tablespoon Dijon mustard	Ground black pepper to taste
1/4 cup maple syrup	2 teaspoons minced garlic	1 tablespoon cornstarch
1/4 cup chopped onions*	1/4 teaspoon ground cinnamon	2 tablespoons cold water
1/4 cup cider vinegar	1/4 teaspoon ground cloves	Salt to taste
1 tablespoon Worcestershire sauce	4 pounds beef short ribs	

Heat broiler to high heat.**

Combine the first nine ingredients in a small bowl and set aside.

Cut ribs into individual serving-size pieces. Place in a roasting pan and sprinkle with pepper. Broil 4 to 6 inches from the heat for 3 to 5 minutes on each side or until browned. Remove from the oven and place on paper towels.

Place ribs in a 5-quart slow cooker, topping with the tomato juice mixture. Cover and cook on low for 6 to 7 hours or until meat pulls easily away from the bone. If you do not have access to a slow cooker, place all the ingredients into a 5-quart ovenproof pan and bring up to a simmer on the stove. Cover and place in a 275° F oven and cook for 2 to 3 hours or until the meat is tender and pulls away from the bone easily.

In a small bowl, combine cornstarch and cold water until the mixture is smooth. Remove ribs from the slow cooker or oven and reserve. Skim fat off the sauce and discard. Bring sauce to a boil and stir in cornstarch mixture. Return to a boil and cook until the sauce thickens.

Season with salt and pepper to taste. Spoon sauce over ribs before serving.

Note: Serve with mashed potatoes and braised root vegetables.

* Chopping should yield 1/4-inch pieces.

** If you don't have a broiler, the ribs can be browned in a pan over medium-high heat. Be sure to coat the bottom of the pan with oil to prevent the meat from sticking.

Chocolate Caramel Nut Cheesecake

Wickedly delicious, this cheesecake is one of the most sought-after dessert creations in the Sportservice repertoire. This recipe is perfect for those times when you need something rich and luscious.

Prep time: 8 minutes
Cook time: 85 minutes
Yields: 1 (9-inch) cheesecake

4 tablespoons melted, unsalted butter	3 (8-ounce) packages softened cream cheese	2 chopped king-size Snickers candy bars
1 1/4 cups graham cracker crumbs	3 eggs	
3/4 cup plus 1 tablespoon granulated sugar	2 teaspoons vanilla extract	

Preheat oven to 350° F.

In a small bowl, combine the melted butter, graham cracker crumbs and 1 tablespoon granulated sugar. Press into the bottom of a 9-inch springform pan.

Bake for 10 minutes or until crisp.

Using an electric stand mixer, cream 3/4 cup of sugar and cream cheese together until smooth, scraping the bowl often. Add the eggs one at a time, thoroughly scraping the bowl after each egg is incorporated. Add the vanilla. Fold in chopped candy bar and pour cheesecake batter into baked crust.*

Bake for 60 minutes or until a toothpick comes out clean. Set in refrigerator overnight. Carefully remove the springform pan's sides.

Serve chilled.

*Batter should be smooth. If you have lumps, strain through a sieve before adding the candy pieces.

Because cheesecake incorporates beaten eggs that coagulate, the top often splits when it is cooling. To avoid this, try placing the pan in a hot-water bath while baking to ensure even heating. Another method involves baking the cheesecake at a lower temperature and, after turning the oven off, allowing the cheesecake to cool in the oven with the door slightly open. If all else fails, try a scrumptious solution: Top the dessert with berries or whipped cream.

Venezia Bruschetta

This chunky tomato spread is an ideal match for thin slices of Italian bread. Oregano, basil, parsley and Parmesan cheese combine to give it just the right flavor. Serve as an appetizer at any get-together or dinner party.

Prep time: 13 minutes
Cook time: 10 minutes
Yields: 6 servings

4 cups diced, vine-ripened tomatoes
  (approximately 3 to 4 tomatoes)*

1/4 cup diced, sweet, red onion*

2 tablespoons olive oil

1 tablespoon minced, fresh oregano

1 teaspoon minced, fresh basil

2 teaspoons minced, fresh Italian parsley

Salt to taste

Ground black pepper to taste

1 baguette (approximately 18 inches long)
  cut into 1-inch slices

1/4 cup shredded Parmesan cheese

Preheat oven to 375° F.

In a medium bowl, combine tomatoes, onion, olive oil, oregano, basil, parsley, salt and pepper. Place bread slices on a baking sheet, topping each slice with the tomato mixture. Sprinkle with Parmesan cheese. Bake in preheated oven for 8 to 10 minutes or until bottom of bread is lightly browned. Cool 5 minutes before serving.

Note: To prevent the bread from becoming soggy, lay slices on a baking tray and brush lightly with olive oil. Season bread with salt and pepper and toast in a 350° F oven until lightly browned. Or just grill lightly to "mark" the bread before spooning the tomato mixture on top.

*Dicing should yield 1/4-inch pieces.

DALLAS/ARLINGTON

Rangers Ballpark in Arlington

Probably the first thing anyone needs to know about Rangers Ballpark in Arlington is that residents near the stadium refer to it only as "The Ballpark." Granted, there are numerous other venues around the country from which to watch baseball, but according to Texas Rangers fans, only their stadium is worthy of the title.

Rangers Ballpark in Arlington truly is a special place. Built in just 23 months, the 49,115-seat stadium offers one of the most complete baseball experiences in the country. It includes a baseball museum, children's learning center and baseball park. Numerous lakes and outdoor green spaces surround the perimeter of the stadium.

Fans who visit The Ballpark will recognize the stadium as a strong representation of its home state. Lone Stars are present in the concourses and on many of the seat aisles. An asymmetrical playing field and a home run porch in right field help make watching a Rangers game an intimate experience.

That's good news for fans, considering how many big names and teams have made their way through Texas. Nolan Ryan pitched two of his seven no-hitters while wearing a Rangers uniform. Ivan "Pudge" Rodriguez was a 10-time all-star while in Texas. The Rangers even made three trips to the postseason from 1996 to 1999, and in 2007, caught the nation's attention by breaking a league record for the number of runs scored in a game.

With a gem of a stadium to call their own and enough excitement to go around, there is nowhere Rangers fans would rather be.

Prawns with Boursin Cheese
wrapped in Smoked Apple Bacon with Chipotle Remoulade

Be sure not to call a prawn a shrimp. While the two sea creatures look similar, each has its own distinct taste. This recipe caters to the flavors of the prawn, complementing it with soft and creamy Boursin cheese.

Prep time: 8 minutes
Cook time: 20 minutes
Yields: 6 servings

6 large peeled and deveined tail-on prawns*

6 large slices smoked apple bacon

1/4 cup fine breadcrumbs

6 ounces Boursin cheese

Salt to taste

Ground black pepper to taste

1/3 cup white wine

1 cup Chipotle Remoulade (see below)

Preheat oven to 325° F.

Butterfly the prawns, cutting from the back to the front and leaving each tail on. Refrigerate until needed.

Partially cook the bacon on a baking sheet for 8 to 10 minutes in the preheated oven.

Combine the breadcrumbs with cheese and divide into six equal portions.

Place the Boursin cheese mixture inside each prawn and wrap with a slice of bacon. Lay the prawns on a sheet pan coated with nonstick cooking spray.

Season with salt and pepper and a splash of white wine. Bake for 12 to 15 minutes or until the bacon is fully cooked.

Serve prawns hot with a dollop of Chipotle Remoulade as an appetizer or entrée.

*Approximately 12 per pound.

Chipotle Remoulade

Prep time: 5 minutes
Yields: 1 1/2 cups

1 cup mayonnaise

1 1/2 teaspoons finely chopped red onion

1 teaspoon finely sliced green onion

1 teaspoon pickle relish

Juice from 1 lemon

1/2 teaspoon chopped capers

1 1/2 tablespoons Chipotle Base (see next page)

Salt to taste

Ground black pepper to taste

Combine all ingredients in a small bowl and season to taste with salt and pepper. Cover and refrigerate until needed.

Chipotle Base

Prep time: 5 minutes
Cook time: 7 minutes
Yields: 2 1/4 cups

3/4 cup canned chipotle peppers
  packed in adobo sauce

1/4 cup chopped yellow onion

2 cloves minced, fresh garlic

1/2 cup red wine

Salt to taste

1 cup water

Mix all ingredients in a saucepan and bring to a boil. Reduce the heat and simmer
for 5 minutes. Remove from heat and let cool. Once cool, mix in a bar blender
until mixture becomes a purée. Strain through a fine strainer.

Cover tightly and refrigerate.

Tia Maria Mexican Flan

A little Tia Maria liqueur poured over this traditional Mexican dessert makes all the difference in its flavor. A perfect fit for Rangers Ballpark, it will allow everyone to taste Mexican flavors at home.

Prep time: 30 minutes
Cook time: 1 hour, 30 minutes
Yields: 1 (9-inch) pan

3/4 cup granulated sugar

4 egg yolks

1 tablespoon vanilla extract

1/8 cup Tia Maria liqueur (can also use Kahlúa)

3/4 cup half-and-half

1 1/2 cups whole milk

1 (3-ounce) can sweetened condensed milk

Preheat oven to 275° F.

Place 3/4 cup of the granulated sugar in a medium sauté pan and place over medium heat until sugar becomes syrup-like. Pour caramelized sugar quickly into the bottom of a 9-inch pan. Set aside.

Place egg yolks, vanilla and Tia Maria in a small bowl and mix using a whisk.

Gradually add the half-and-half, whole milk and condensed milk to the egg mixture. Ensure all ingredients are mixed well.

Pour the mixture into the 9-inch pan (with the caramelized sugar on the bottom). Set in a shallow pan and pour hot water one-quarter of the way up the sides of the 9-inch pan.

Bake uncovered for approximately 1 1/2 hours or until a knife inserted in the center comes out clean.

Remove the flan from the water bath and cool to room temperature. Chill in the refrigerator for 2 to 3 hours. When ready to serve, dip the pie pan quickly in hot water, then invert on a serving dish. Cut in wedges and serve decorated with fresh whipped cream and chocolate syrup.

DETROIT

Comerica Park

Detroit baseball stadiums have a special place in the history of Delaware North Companies Sportservice. In 1930, when the sports concessions giant was nothing more than three hardworking young men with an age-old dream, the Jacobs brothers won a contract at Tiger Stadium. Their first in the majors.

Many workers at what is now a $2 billion global hospitality and food service company can recount the story of how L.M. Jacobs – the present-day chairman's father – boarded a train in Buffalo to return to Tigers owner Frank Navin the portion of the profit Jacobs thought was excessive.

The large measure of integrity has paid for itself countless times in helping to create the culture of Sportservice and in laying the foundation for the long and successful relationship the company has shared with professional sports. Even today, Delaware North continues to fulfill its promise of bringing the best culinary tastes and trends to Detroit fans every year.

One thing that has changed about the relationship is the place the Detroit Tigers call home. In 1997, a shovelful of dirt marked the beginning of today's Comerica Park. It is a modern stadium filled with all of the bells and whistles meant to give fans the ultimate in live entertainment. A mammoth water feature located in the center field can be choreographed to any music, and on the main concourse, pedestrians can enjoy a decade-by-decade look at baseball.

When it comes to satisfying tastes, Comerica Park is one of the best stadiums in the world. While typical ballparks have a point of sale for every 200 fans, Comerica Park has one for every 125. Among these choices are the Brushfire Grill, a barbecue spot behind third base, and the Big Cat Food Court adjacent to first base.

It is a stadium fit for a team that has collected four World Series titles in its history and had legends like Ty Cobb and Hank Greenberg running its bases.

It is filled with Delaware North memories, too. For more than three-quarters of a century, the two organizations have followed the same guiding principle: giving fans the absolute best in ballpark experiences.

79

Avocado Crema Fresca

Sometimes called the alligator pear, an avocado is a rough, green-skinned fruit. Combined with all the ingredients that go into this spread, the avocado tastes smooth and delicious. Use this recipe for a cool, flavorful topping during the summer season.

Prep time: 5 to 7 minutes
Yields: 1 1/2 cups

1/2 bunch washed and dried cilantro	1 cup sour cream
1 ripe avocado	Juice from 2 limes

Clean cilantro and pick off leaves. Peel avocado and remove seed.

Combine all ingredients in a food processor and purée, or mix with a whisk or a fork.

Note: Serve with any fish, chicken or chips.

Boursin Chicken Baguette

A newer addition to the menu at Comerica Park, these mini treats pack an assortment of flavors into every bite. They can be served as an appetizer or as a snack.

Prep time: 10 minutes
Cook time: 12 minutes
Yields: 8 sandwiches

1 cup balsamic or Greek vinaigrette	8 ounces herb Boursin cheese	3 tablespoons vinaigrette dressing
4 (6-ounce) boneless, skinless chicken breasts	4 sliced yellow and red vine-ripened tomatoes	
1 French baguette	2 ounces frisée or spring mix lettuce	

Marinate chicken in balsamic or Greek vinaigrette in refrigerator for at least 2 hours.

Preheat grill to medium. Place chicken on the grill and cook until internal temperature reaches 165° F. Set aside.

Warm baguette slightly (optional). Slice baguette and chicken breast lengthwise.

Spread Boursin cheese on inside of top and bottom of baguette. Place sliced chicken on bottom of baguette.

Gently mix tomatoes with lettuce and vinaigrette. Place salad mixture on baguette. Slice baguette diagonally into eight portions. Serve with potato chips.

Boursin cheese was created in 1957 by Francois Boursin in Normandy, France. Similar in texture to American cream cheese, it comes in a variety of flavors, including garlic and herb, his first.

Eggplant Rollatini

An Indian legend tells of a traveler who ate a raw eggplant and grew very ill. This story resulted in the vegetable being called the "mad apple" and considered poisonous in many parts of the world. Fortunately, the chefs at Comerica Park don't feel that way. They use it in this delicious dish, which can easily be prepared in a home kitchen.

Prep time: 25 minutes
Cook time: 25 to 30 minutes
Yields: 6 servings

1 large eggplant

1/4 teaspoon salt plus additional to taste

1/4 teaspoon ground black pepper
    plus additional to taste

1 cup all-purpose flour

3 eggs

1 cup milk

2 1/2 cups Italian breadcrumbs

2 cups olive oil

1 (24-ounce) jar marinara sauce (any brand)

1 cup heavy cream

1/2 cup pesto sauce

1/2 cup Parmesan cheese

8 ounces cooked linguini

1/2 cup Romano cheese

2 ounces fresh basil (optional)

Preheat oven to 375° F.

Wash eggplant and slice lengthwise into 1/4-inch-thick pieces. (This should yield approximately 12 to 15 slices.) Season with salt and let sit 30 minutes or until much of the moisture is extracted. Rinse eggplant slices under cold, running water and pat dry.

Add 1/4 teaspoon of salt and pepper to flour.

Whisk eggs with milk for egg wash.

Dredge the eggplant slices first in seasoned flour, then egg wash and lastly, in the Italian breadcrumbs. Set aside.

Heat oil in a large skillet over medium-high heat. Cook eggplant 1 minute per side or until browned. Transfer to a pan lined with paper towels to absorb excess oil. Reserve until needed.

In a medium saucepan, heat marinara sauce over medium heat until warmed through. Keep warm until needed.

Combine heavy cream and pesto sauce in a small saucepan and cook over medium heat. When mixture is hot, stir in Parmesan cheese until melted. Adjust seasoning with salt and pepper. Keep the sauce warm until needed.

Cook linguini in boiling, salted water until al dente. Drain, but don't rinse. Set aside.

When ready to assemble dish, toss linguini with pesto cream sauce.

Ladle a small amount of marinara sauce into the bottom of a medium casserole dish. Lay eggplant out on a cutting board and place a small amount of linguini on top of each slice. Roll eggplant and place in the casserole dish. Repeat until all of the eggplant has been rolled.

Top with the remaining marinara sauce. Sprinkle with Romano cheese and bake for 25 minutes or until the cheese is bubbling and the eggplant is tender.

Sprinkle with chopped fresh basil and serve hot.

Chocolate Crêpe Batter

Often referred to as thin pancakes, crêpes pack much more flavor than one might think. This chocolate crêpe batter is perfect for an early morning surprise or a romantic treat.

Prep time: 10 minutes
Cook time: 20 minutes
Yields: 6 cups batter; 24 crêpes

1/2 cup cocoa	1/2 cup granulated sugar	1/4 cup vanilla extract
1 1/3 cups all-purpose flour	8 eggs	1/4 cup vegetable oil
3/4 teaspoon salt	3 1/4 cups whole milk	

Combine all dry ingredients in a bowl and set aside.

Whisk eggs, milk and vanilla. Add the dry mixture to the wet mixture and mix well.

Lightly grease a nonstick 7-inch sauté pan with vegetable oil and place over medium heat.

Ladle 1/4 cup of batter into the pan and turn pan to coat the entire bottom and a small amount of the sides.

Cook slightly until the crêpe batter begins to take on color. Carefully turn it out on a warm sheet tray. (Note: Cook only one side of the crêpe.)

Lay out finished shells on a lined sheet tray and separate layers with bakery sheet liners to prevent the crêpes from sticking together.

Wrap immediately and refrigerate until ready to use. The shells may be kept for four days in the refrigerator or for 30 days in the freezer.*

*You may extend shelf life by storing in a corrugated box while frozen.

Unable to grow enough wheat to make bread, the residents of Brittany, a northwest region of France, invented a delightful alternative: crêpes. There are two types of crêpes: sweet crêpes, which are made with wheat flour and slightly sweetened, and savory galettes, made with buckwheat flour and unsweetened.

EDMONTON

Rexall Place

Just before entering Rexall Place, Edmonton Oilers fans are reminded they are about to step into a place replete with hockey legends and memories. A large bronze statue of Canadian titan and former Oilers Captain Wayne Gretzky makes sure fans don't miss the point.

There are many things that make Rexall Place a unique arena, not the least of which is the fact that it's the only one where home team players actually walk through the lower concourse – adjacent to the club bar – to get to the ice. Also adding to the mystique of Rexall Place are the retired jerseys that hang in the rafters. Those of Gretzky, Mark Messier and Paul Coffey. Names that tell the story of hockey at its finest.

Originally known as the Northlands Coliseum and later dubbed both the Edmonton Coliseum and the Skyreach Centre, Rexall Place currently has

room for 16,839 fans and 67 luxury suites. That's more than enough space for spectators to take in Oilers games or cheer on the Edmonton Rush of the National Lacrosse League, while feasting on numerous culinary choices.

The venue has hosted myriad major events, including the 1978 Commonwealth Games and part of the Universiade in 1983. Annually, the Canadian Finals Rodeo visits the arena.

All of this adds up to Rexall Place's unofficial ranking as a one-of-a-kind venue that breathes excitement. And from time to time, quite a racket. Oilers fans' cheers in games 3, 4 and 6 of the 2006 Stanley Cup finals reached 114 decibels, a reliable indication of the passion Edmonton fans have for their team and the world-class arena it calls home.

Bison Tenderloin

It's difficult to find fault with Buffalo meat. It brings the same full-bodied taste that beef does, but with healthier benefits. Having less fat and cholesterol than most cuts of beef, bison meat is packed with delicious flavor.

Prep time: 15 minutes
Cook time: 40 minutes
Yields: 8 servings

Vegetable oil to sear tenderloin

1 (3-pound) bison tenderloin*

1/2 cup vegetable oil

1 tablespoon seasoning salt

1 tablespoon onion powder

1 tablespoon garlic salt

1/2 tablespoon ground black pepper

1 tablespoon Montreal Steak Seasoning

1 tablespoon ketchup

1 tablespoon steak sauce

Pour oil to coat the bottom of a pan large enough to hold the tenderloin and heat it over medium-high heat. When oil is hot, sear the bison tenderloin on all sides until it's golden brown. Remove from heat. Allow to cool.

Combine remaining ingredients in a bowl and mix. Rub mixture into tenderloin and let rest for 30 minutes at room temperature, followed by 6 hours in the refrigerator.

Roast at 300° F for 25 to 30 minutes or until internal temperature reaches 125° F (medium-rare). Let rest for 10 minutes before carving.

Serve with fresh rolls, grainy German mustard, butter and horseradish.

*Ask your meat cutter to make the tenderloin oven ready.

Rexall Cured Salmon

The curing process used by Rexall chefs involves a dry rub of salt and/or sugar with an assortment of herbs. This mixture is then rubbed onto the surface of the meat and put aside for a number of days. The salt-and-sugar mixture draws large amounts of liquid from the fish, replacing it with the seasoning. It's a long process, but Oilers fans can attest to the fact that it's worth the wait.

Prep time: 20 minutes plus 48 hours for curing
Yields: 48 servings (enough for a cocktail party)

1 cup coarse salt	1/2 cup white rum	1/2 cup white wine
1 cup brown sugar	2 (2-pound) salmon filets	1/2 thinly sliced English cucumber
Zest of 2 limes	2 uncooked and grated large red beets	3 tablespoons white balsamic vinegar
2 tablespoons roasted and crushed black peppercorns	1 julienned, large Maui or Vidalia onion	
8 torn mint leaves	1/2 cup granulated sugar	

Mix salt, brown sugar, lime zest, peppercorns, mint leaves and white rum into a paste.

Thoroughly coat salmon with the paste, applying one-third on the underside and two-thirds on top.

Wrap salmon tightly in plastic wrap and cure for 24 hours in refrigerator.

Remove fish from the refrigerator and unwrap the plastic. Rinse and pat the salmon dry.

Cover with the red beets and cure in refrigerator for an additional 24 hours.

Before serving, braise onions in sugar and white wine. Remove from heat and set aside to cool. Toss cucumbers with balsamic vinegar.

Remove salmon from refrigerator. Place on a platter and slice thinly. Serve with sliced baguettes, braised onions and cucumbers.

In addition to being a wonderfully versatile fish, salmon also has a rich and colorful history. According to Norse mythology, when the god of mischief and strife killed the god of beauty and light, he jumped into the river and transformed himself into a salmon in order to escape punishment from other gods. When a trap was set out to catch him, he attempted to leap over it, but was caught by a god who grabbed him by the tail. This caused his tail to stretch, giving us at least one explanation for why salmon have long, tapered tails.

Banana Spring Rolls

Edmonton's Chinese Spring Festival is held in accordance with the Chinese New Year, which occurs on the first day of the first lunar month. This means that the holiday can fall on a different day every year. One thing that doesn't change about the festival is the high quantity of spring rolls that are consumed during the day.

Prep time: 10 to 12 minutes
Cook time: 20 minutes
Yields: 6 spring rolls

1 quart vegetable oil (for frying)	1 tablespoon fresh calamansi or lime juice	1/2 cup buko shreds (young coconut)
2 tablespoons butter	3 firm, ripe bananas	Vanilla ice cream
1/4 cup brown sugar	6 spring roll wrappers	

Preheat vegetable oil in a deep fryer to 350° F.

Melt butter in a small pan over medium heat and add brown sugar and juice. Bring to a simmer. Keep warm and set aside.

Slice bananas in half lengthwise and then in half crosswise. Place two pieces on each spring roll wrapper. Add buko shreds and drizzle with brown sugar mixture.

Prepare as you would a spring roll, folding edges in and rolling, using water to seal edges.

Deep fry spring rolls for 2 minutes. Remove from oil and place on a plate lined with paper towels to absorb excess oil.

Cut each spring roll on the bias and present on a plate with vanilla ice cream.

The banana plant is one of the most usable plants in the world. That is, very little goes to waste. The flower is a common ingredient in Southeast Asian and Indian cuisine, while the fruit is delicious on its own or in a variety of desserts. A banana plant can produce approximately 20 bananas before dying and being replaced by a new growth.

Saskatoon Flan

The Saskatoon Flan does not hail from the great city of Saskatoon. Instead, this dessert gets its name from saskatoon berries that are native to Canada's prairie provinces. These flavors blend themselves into the interior of this dessert and produce a wonderful finish to any meal.

Prep time: 30 minutes
Cook time: 70 to 80 minutes
Yields: 1 (10-inch) serving

FOR THE CRUST

1 1/2 cups all-purpose flour

1 1/2 tablespoons baking powder

1/2 cup butter

1/2 cup granulated sugar

1 egg

1 1/2 teaspoons almond extract

1/4 tablespoon salt

FOR THE FLAN

4 cups frozen saskatoons

2 tablespoons Grand Marnier

1 tablespoon grated lemon zest

2 cups sour cream

1 cup cream cheese

8 egg yolks

1/2 cup granulated sugar

1 1/2 tablespoons almond extract

1/4 cup minute tapioca

Preheat oven to 325° F.

Sift flour and baking powder and set aside.

In a separate bowl, cream butter and sugar. Add egg and almond extract.

Slowly add dry ingredients, mixing just until blended. Press gently on bottom and 2 inches up the sides of a 10-inch springform pan, making a 1/4-inch-thick crust. Let rest for 10 to 20 minutes before filling and baking.

Combine saskatoons, Grand Marnier and lemon zest. Pour evenly over crust.

Combine all remaining ingredients in a bowl and pour evenly over saskatoons.

Bake for 70 to 80 minutes. Check for doneness by inserting a toothpick or bamboo skewer in the center. If it comes out clean, the flan is done. Let cool and place in refrigerator overnight to set.

FRISCO

Dr Pepper Ballpark

When Dr Pepper Ballpark opened in 2003 as the home of the Class AA Frisco RoughRiders baseball team, it earned the distinction of best new baseball stadium from baseballparks.com. And despite the fact a few years have passed since then, 'Riders fans — as they are known in these parts — continue to believe it deserves the distinction.

With the look and feel of a small town on the move, Dr Pepper Ballpark fits right in with Frisco, the fast-growing northern suburb of the Dallas/ Fort Worth megapolis that is known for its strong sense of community. Want to stay anonymous? Don't move to Frisco, where you're likely to run into friends and neighbors while walking your dog, meandering down the aisles of the grocery store or — needless to say — while at a 'Riders game. In fact, take a break from the up-close-and-personal view the stadium's seating bowl offers and give San Juan Hill behind the home run fence a whirl. You'll be surrounded by others relaxing on the grass and picnicking during the game.

The Frisco RoughRiders is a farm league team for the Texas Rangers that often has future MLB stars working their way through the organization. Such talent helps the team contend for Texas South Division Titles on a regular basis and keeps loyal fans hungry for the kind of experience they have come to expect from Dr Pepper Ballpark.

Herb-Crusted Pork Loin
with Mustard and Caraway

Originating in Europe and parts of Western Asia, caraway is a spice highly regarded for putting any recipe over the top. It's truly the finishing touch for this dish that calls on many seasonings to create one great flavor.

Prep time: 15 minutes
Cook time: 1 hour
Yields: 6 servings

1 (2 1/2- to 3-pound) boneless center-cut pork loin	1/3 cup olive oil	1 1/2 teaspoons minced, fresh thyme leaves
1/4 cup breadcrumbs	Salt to taste	1 teaspoon whole-grain mustard
1/4 cup grated Parmesan cheese	Ground black pepper to taste	1 teaspoon toasted caraway seeds
1 teaspoon minced garlic	1 teaspoon minced garlic	1/4 cup chopped, fresh basil

Preheat oven to 325° F.

Beginning 1/2 inch from one end of the pork loin, cut a pocket lengthwise, stopping approximately 1/2 inch before the opposite end.

Mix breadcrumbs with half of the Parmesan cheese, garlic and 1 tablespoon of olive oil. Mix until crumbs are evenly coated with oil. Season to taste with salt and pepper.

In a small bowl, combine 2 tablespoons of olive oil, remaining Parmesan cheese, garlic, thyme, mustard, caraway seeds and basil. Mix until smooth and paste-like. Season with salt and pepper.

Spread one-half of mustard/caraway paste in loin pocket and tie with butcher's twine. Season loin with salt and pepper.

Heat 2 tablespoons of olive oil in a large skillet Add roast, turning frequently until all sides are browned.

Remove twine from roast. Spread remaining herb paste over loin and top with breadcrumb mixture.

Place on a baking pan with a rack and transfer to the oven.

Cook for 1 hour or until internal temperature reaches 155° F. Remove from oven and let rest for 10 to 15 minutes. Carve into 1/2-inch slices and serve immediately.

Note: Serve with whole-grain mustard and pork jus. Sautéed apple slices mixed with dried cranberries make a delicious and attractive garnish.

MILWAUKEE

Miller Park

Forget America's pastime for a minute. The greatest tribute to sausages takes place whenever the Brewers are in town.

At the end of the sixth inning of every game in Miller Park, a tradition called the Sausage Race pits a bratwurst, an Italian sausage, a Polish sausage, a chorizo and a hot dog against one another in a race around the perimeter of the field. That's when fans root for their favorite sausage, getting on their feet to see which piece of meat will conquer the course in the least amount of time.

The racers are Miller Park employees who don oversized costumes before taking the field to keep alive a tradition that celebrates the love these fans have for their links. Indeed, Miller Park is the only ballpark in the majors where the hot dog (the edible variety, that is) is not top dog. Bratwurst loaded with Secret Stadium Sauce is the big seller in Milwaukee.

It's also a symbol of how much Brewers fans love coming to their home team's ballpark. Opened in 2001, Miller Park has some of the best amenities in baseball. A convertible roof canvasses the stadium and allows games to be played outdoors and indoors. The Metavante Club is one of the finest stadium restaurants in baseball, where fans can try fine-dining cuisine along with their beloved brats.

The action on the field usually isn't all that bad either. The owners of the 1982 American League Pennant, the Brewers are a constant and formidable force in the National League Central. Such baseball greats as Robin Yount, Paul Molitor, Jeremy Burnitz and Cecil Cooper have left their marks on the organization.

Crab and Shrimp Ceviche
on a Spoon

Ceviche is a form of citrus-marinated seafood salad that originated in Peru. Teamed up with crab and shrimp, this dish is a favorite high-end offering for Brewers fans and a perfect entrée for a dinner party, especially when it's dressed up with fresh cilantro or caviar.

Prep time: 30 minutes
Marinating time: 2 hours
Yields: 6 servings

1/2 pound drained lump crab meat
 (or any crab desired)
12 peeled, cooked and shelled small shrimp
1/4 cup fresh lime juice
1/4 cup plus 1 tablespoon fresh lemon juice

1/4 cup fresh orange juice
1/2 cup canned tomato juice
1 teaspoon horseradish
1/2 teaspoon Cholula Hot Sauce
 (or your favorite hot sauce)
1/4 cup chopped cilantro

Salt to taste
Ground black pepper to taste
1 diced avocado
1/4 cup julienned red onion
1 tablespoon olive oil

Place crab and shrimp in separate small bowls.

Mix 1/4 cup lemon juice, orange juice, tomato juice, horseradish, Cholula, cilantro, and desired amount of salt and pepper in a blender. Pour half of the liquid over the crab and half over the shrimp. Marinate in the refrigerator for 2 hours.

Place diced avocado in a small bowl. Add remaining lemon to it so it doesn't lose its color.

Place a small sauté pan over medium heat. Add oil, then onion and cook for 10 minutes or until onion is very soft. Allow to cool.

After 2 hours, strain ceviche liquid from crab and shrimp. Discard liquid. Place a small amount of avocado, onion, crab and shrimp on a tablespoon. Serve.

Note: Ceviche can also be served on crackers, flat bread or crostini bread.

Stadium Bratwurst

Miller Park is the only professional baseball stadium in North America where the frankfurter plays second fiddle to another meat dish. Brewers fans are proud of the anomaly, celebrating it with the famous sausage races. When traveling to Milwaukee, be sure to try one of the signature links topped with sauerkraut, caramelized onions and a generous portion of Secret Stadium Sauce.

Prep time: 5 minutes
Cook time: 20 minutes
Yields: 6 servings

6 precooked bratwurst	1 cup sauerkraut
2 generic bock beers	1/2 cup caramelized onions
Secret Stadium Sauce	

In a medium saucepan over medium-low heat, slowly bring beer to a simmer. Cook bratwurst for 15 minutes. Remove from beer.

Place in a sauté pan over medium-high heat for 2 1/2 minutes on each side or until browned.

Served topped with Secret Stadium Sauce, sauerkraut and caramelized onions.

Pork Adobada

"Adobo" is the Spanish word for seasoning or marinade. Anything that has been marinated with an adobo is said to be adobada. In this recipe, pork is the lucky meat that gets covered in this smooth, delicious seasoning. Don't be surprised if after making this recipe you're not trying to make a few more things adobada.

Prep time: 10 minutes plus marinating time (4 hours)
Cook time: 80 minutes
Yields: 8 servings

1 (48-ounce) pork shoulder	3 tablespoons chipotle pepper purée	1/4 cup oil
1/2 cup orange juice concentrate	2 tablespoons ground cumin	Kosher salt to taste
1/2 cup pineapple juice concentrate	1/2 cup apple cider vinegar	

Cut pork into three large pieces. Mix all other ingredients into a paste and rub well into meat. Place in refrigerator 4 hours or overnight.

Roast uncovered in 350° F oven for 30 to 40 minutes. Cover and roast another 30 to 40 minutes or until the meat is "fork tender." Pull meat into small servings.

Serve with flour tortillas and salsa, limes, chopped cilantro and diced onions.

Spanish Rice

Spanish rice is like a best friend…easy to be with and always fun to have around. This side dish goes well with everything from meat dishes to tortillas and even salads. Simple to make and delicious to eat, this recipe always delivers.

Prep time: 10 minutes
Cook time: 50 minutes
Yields: 6 cups

3 cups roughly chopped plum tomatoes	1 medium ear of corn	2 cups long-grain rice
1/2 cup roughly chopped Spanish onion	(can use canned or frozen kernels)	Kosher salt to taste
1 garlic clove	4 tablespoons olive oil	Freshly ground black pepper to taste
4 cups chicken stock (or broth)	1/4 cup small-diced carrot	2 tablespoons butter

Preheat oven to 325° F for roasting corn.

Purée tomatoes, onions and garlic in half of the chicken stock and set aside.

Wash corn. Rub with olive oil or butter, and roast in preheated oven for 10 to 12 minutes. Gently remove kernels from the cob using a paring knife.

Add olive oil to a medium skillet and sauté carrots for 3 minutes over medium heat. Add roasted corn and sauté for an additional 2 minutes. Add rice and continue to cook for 5 minutes or until rice is golden in color. Add tomato purée mixture and cook for 3 minutes to coat rice, stirring constantly.

Add remaining half of the chicken stock. Cover and simmer for 30 minutes. Season with kosher salt and freshly ground pepper to taste. Gently stir butter in rice.

NASHVILLE

Sommet Center

Designers of the Sommet Center saw to it that everything about the facility serves as a tribute to the great city of Nashville and its strong musical roots, including its entrance at the site of the original home of the Grand Ole Opry.

That detail is just the beginning of the significance of this state-of-the-art live entertainment venue. One of the most massive sports complexes in the nation, the Sommet Center features a 22-story tower that also houses the Nashville Convention & Visitors Bureau, the Tennessee Sports Hall of Fame and two theaters. Four levels of seating enable fans to get close to the action and 72 luxury suites make it a whole lot more comfortable.

Now the home of the NHL's Nashville Predators and the Arena Football League's Nashville Kats, Sommet Center often gets called upon to host large events. It's a regular stop for the NCAA Men's Basketball Tournament and even welcomed the 1997 U.S. National Figure Skating Championship.

Because the venue draws so many fans, it has also been a catalyst for numerous other projects downtown, including the Country Music Hall of Fame and the Frist Center for the Visual Arts. Since the team's first year in 1998, the Nashville Predators franchise has progressed and improved every season, making appearances in the 2004, 2006 and 2007 NHL playoffs.

Hummus

A concoction of chickpeas, sesame tahini, lemon juice and garlic, hummus is a healthy, one-of-a-kind sauce that originated in the Middle East and can be served in many ways. Often used as a spread for flat bread, hummus can also serve as a dip for tortilla chips or stand alone as part of an entrée.

Prep time: 10 minutes
Yields: 3 cups

1 (15-ounce) can drained garbanzo beans	2 ounces Tahini paste	Ground black pepper to taste
1 cup roasted garlic cloves (see below)	1/2 cup olive oil	
Juice of 1/2 fresh lemon	Salt to taste	

Using a food processor, purée all ingredients into a smooth paste. Adjust seasoning if needed. Spoon into a bowl and serve with crackers, grilled pita or crudités.

Roasted Garlic

Cook time: 1 hour
Yields: 1 roasted garlic bulb

1 garlic bulb

Olive oil

Preheat oven to 350° F. Cut top off of garlic bulb. Drizzle olive oil over top.

Wrap garlic in foil and roast for 45 minutes to 1 hour or until garlic is golden brown and tender. Take out what you need and reserve the rest for bread, mashed potatoes, etc.

Sugar and Spice Salmon

with Scallion Crushed Potatoes and Tomato Relish

A fine blend of sugars and spices makes this recipe distinctive. Nashville Predators fans look forward to this dish in Sommet Center's fine dining sections.

Prep time: 5 minutes
Cook time: 10 minutes
Yields: 4 servings

4 (4-ounce) salmon filets	2 tablespoons dried thyme leaf	2 teaspoons onion powder
1 1/2 cups dark brown sugar	1/4 cup kosher salt	1 teaspoon cayenne pepper
1/4 cup paprika	2 tablespoons dustless ground black pepper	
1 tablespoon dried oregano leaf	2 teaspoons garlic powder	

Combine all ingredients and store at room temperature in an airtight container.

Preheat oven to 400° F.

Lightly coat a shallow roasting pan with nonstick spray.

Coat the top of the salmon well with sugar-and-spice mixture. Place salmon filets in prepared roasting pan. Bake salmon for 7 to 10 minutes or until it flakes easily with a fork.

Serve hot on a bed of Scallion Crushed Potatoes and top with Tomato Relish.

Scallion Crushed Potatoes

Prep time: 5 minutes
Cook time: 35 to 40 minutes
Yields: 1 1/2 cups

1 pound Yukon Gold potatoes	2 tablespoons finely diced Spanish onion	Kosher salt to taste
1 tablespoon salt	2 tablespoons thinly sliced scallions	Freshly ground black pepper to taste
1/4 cup olive oil		

Place potatoes in a pot with 1 tablespoon of salt and enough water to cover. Bring to a boil and reduce heat to a simmer. Cook potatoes for 35 to 40 minutes or until they are "fork tender." Drain and return empty pot to the stove.

Reduce heat under pot to low and add a small amount of oil. Sauté diced onions until translucent and aromatic.

Add potatoes and lightly crush into onions with a fork. Fold in scallions and adjust seasoning with kosher salt and fresh, ground black pepper.

Keep warm until needed.

Tomato Relish

Prep time: 15 minutes
Yields: 1 cup

2 cups (small) diced plum tomatoes

2 tablespoons minced red onion

2 finely minced garlic cloves

1 teaspoon red wine vinegar

2 teaspoons olive oil

1 teaspoon chopped, fresh oregano

1 tablespoon chopped, fresh basil

1/2 teaspoon granulated sugar

Kosher salt to taste

Freshly cracked pepper to taste

In a small bowl combine all of the ingredients. Season with salt and pepper.

Refrigerate until needed.

Sweet-n-Sour Wild King Salmon

Hailing from the Pacific Ocean and offering a different taste for salmon aficionados, the Chinook salmon is the breed of fish that is often referred to as "king salmon." This dish is the ultimate special meal.

Prep time: 1 hour, 45 minutes
Cook time: 2 hours
Yields: 8 servings

FOR THE SALMON

1/2 cup sugar

3 tablespoons salt

3 cups warm water

3/8 cup mirin rice wine

8 (4-ounce) skinless center-cut
  wild king salmon filets

Salt to taste

Ground black pepper to taste

1/4 cup olive oil

2 tablespoons sesame oil

FOR THE SAUCE

2 cups mandarin oranges

1 quart orange juice

3/8 cup mirin wine

1/2 cup apricot preserves

2 tablespoons horseradish purée

FOR THE RICE

1 cup Nishiki sushi-style rice

2 cups water

1/4 cup rice wine vinegar

FOR THE GARNISH

8 thinly sliced blood oranges

1 tablespoon sugar

1/4 cup sliced and toasted almonds

1 tablespoon finely diced chives

Preheat oven to 350° F. Place almonds on a flat pan and bake for 5 minutes or until almonds are golden brown.

For the salmon

Combine sugar, salt, warm water and mirin. Mix until salt and sugar are dissolved. Pour over salmon filets and marinate for 1 1/2 hours.

Remove salmon from marinade and pat dry with paper towels. Season with salt and pepper.

Place large sauté pan over medium-high heat. Add olive and sesame oils. When oil mixture is hot, add salmon filets to pan, skin side up, and sear for 2 minutes. Turn and continue to cook for an additional 2 to 3 minutes or until salmon is 75-percent cooked. Remove from pan.

For the sauce

Purée mandarin oranges and add to orange juice along with mirin. Bring to a boil and reduce heat to a simmer. Cook until reduced by half. Strain sauce and return to a simmer.

Add apricot preserves and horseradish and simmer for an additional 20 minutes. Sauce should be a bright amber liquid with a syrup-like consistency. Remove from heat, cover and reserve.

For the rice

Add rice to water. Bring to a boil, reduce heat to a simmer and cover. Cook until water is absorbed. Fluff with a fork and add rice wine vinegar to season. Cover and keep warm.

For the garnish

Preheat oven to 250° F. Lay blood orange slices on a sheet pan lined with parchment paper. Sprinkle with sugar and bake for 1 1/2 hours or until moisture is gone and chips are crisp.

To serve

Place 3 tablespoons of mandarin orange-horseradish reduction on plate. Add a "ball" made with 2 tablespoons of rice to center of plate. Place a blood orange slice on top of rice. Place salmon filet adjacent to the rice and orange slices. Garnish with toasted almonds and chive brunoise.

Baked Apple Pecan Galette

This thin-crust, open-faced apple tart is widely popular around the world as a great end to a delicious meal.

Prep time: 20 minutes
Cook time: 25 minutes
Yields: 4 pies

1 (16-inch-by-20-inch) sheet puff pastry	1/2 cup milk	1/4 cup granulated sugar
1 cup softened cream cheese	3 tablespoons granulated sugar for the puff pastry	2 tablespoons lightly toasted pecans
1/4 cup granulated sugar	3 medium peeled and sliced green apples	
1 teaspoon vanilla	(e.g., Granny Smith)*	
1 egg	1 teaspoon cinnamon	

Preheat oven to 350° F.

Thaw puff pastry.

Mix cream cheese, sugar and vanilla in a small bowl. Reserve until needed.

Combine the egg and milk to form an egg wash. Reserve until needed.

Sprinkle a clean, flat surface with some of the 3 tablespoons of sugar. Roll dough approximately 1/4 inch thick, using more sugar if needed to prevent sticking. Cut rolled dough into 9-inch circles.

"Spike" the dough with a fork to prevent air bubbles from forming in the dough during baking. Invert the dough and brush egg wash onto 1 1/2 inches of the edge. Make an outer lip by rolling and folding the dough edge over itself.

Fill with one-quarter of the cream cheese mixture. Spread evenly on the dough. Layer apple slices evenly over the cheese mixture. Sprinkle with cinnamon and sugar and top with pecans.

Bake for 25 minutes or until crisp and golden brown.

*Slice 1/4 inch thick.

PEORIA

O'Brien Field

O'Brien Field has been a good-luck charm to the Peoria Chiefs and their fans since the first day it opened.

The team's inaugural game in the stadium in 2002 resulted in a 3-0 shutout victory for the Chiefs over Kane County. Building on that strong start, the Chiefs spent the first season racking up 85 wins en route to the best record in team history. The team also earned its best home record ever that year by picking up 47 wins to 24 losses at O'Brien Field.

While the team has cooled down a bit since its first season at O'Brien Field, the Chiefs love nothing better than playing at home. In the stadium's five years of existence, fans saw the minor-league team go 181-148 and 6-1 in the playoffs.

Spectators thrive on taking in a game at the stadium as well. Equipped with 9,600 seats, O'Brien Field brings fans close to the action while offering stunning views of downtown Peoria. Numerous suites offer high-end cuisine and the outdoor picnic plaza is a great place for families to relax and enjoy nine innings of baseball.

This is a place where everyone — including the youngest fans — is at ease. Staff even remember the first fans to step foot in the stadium. It was May 24, 2002, at 2:03 p.m. Chiefs pitcher Tyler Johnson's family entered the stadium and laid their eyes on the Chiefs' new home. From that day forward, O'Brien Field has been a model baseball stadium, catering to fans and players alike.

Beef Tournedoes
with Caramelized Onions and Potato-Wild Mushroom Hash

"Tournedoe" is a French term for a small, round slice of meat taken from the end of the tenderloin. These pieces can then be sautéed or grilled, depending on the chef's preference. Fans of the Peoria Chiefs have come to love this recipe, which combines the tender cut of meat with a bit of brandy and some onions.

Prep time: 40 minutes
Cook time: 10 minutes
Yields: 6 servings

2 tablespoons butter	2 cups heavy cream	12 (2-ounce) beef medallions
4 cups julienned Spanish onion	4 ounces veal glacé	1 pound Potato-Wild Mushroom Hash
1/4 cup finely diced yellow onions	Salt to taste	(see next page)
1/2 cup brandy	Ground black pepper to taste	

To caramelize onions, melt 1 tablespoon butter in a medium sauté pan over medium heat. Add julienned Spanish onions. Reduce heat and cook for 20 to 25 minutes, stirring occasionally, until onions have a deep caramel color.

Meanwhile, melt the remaining tablespoon of butter in a small saucepan. Add diced onions, cooking until they are translucent. Add brandy and reduce by 75 percent.

Add cream and veal glacé. Bring to a simmer over high heat and reduce by 25 percent. Add salt and pepper to taste.

Season beef medallions with salt and pepper and sear on both sides, cooking to 120° F (medium-rare). Let medallions rest for 3 minutes.

Garnish with caramelized onions and serve with Potato-Wild Mushroom Hash. Dress medallions with veal glacé before serving.

Prep time: 15 minutes
Cook time: 40 minutes
Yields: 6 servings

1 pound cubed Yukon gold potatoes	2 tablespoons olive oil to coat	Salt to taste
2 cups sliced crimini mushrooms	1 tablespoon minced, fresh garlic	Ground black pepper to taste
2 cups diced Portobello mushrooms	1 tablespoon stemmed and chopped parsley	

Preheat oven to 375° F.

Mix all ingredients except parsley. Make sure potatoes are coated in olive oil.

Roast for 40 minutes, turning occasionally. When potatoes are turning golden, add parsley. Finish roasting until potatoes are golden brown. Add salt and pepper to taste.

The reproductive upshot of fungi, mushrooms have radiating bladelike structures called gills that produce millions of microscopic spores similar to plant seeds. The color of these spores, ranging from pink to cream, helps to identify the variety of mushroom.

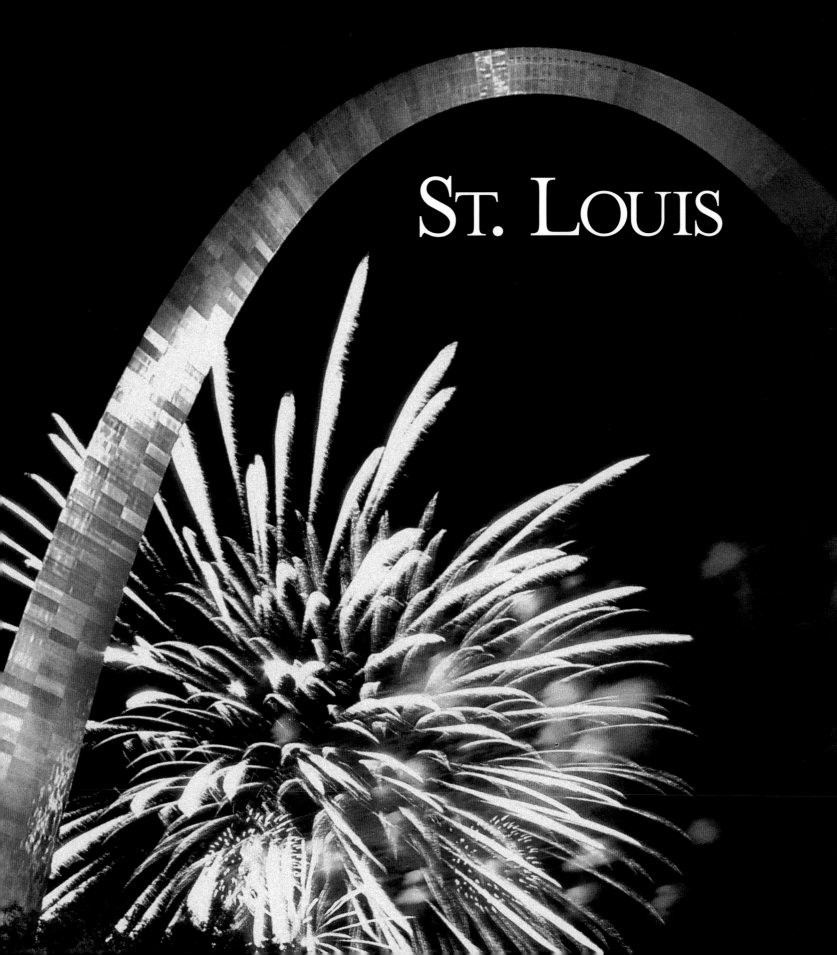

ST. LOUIS

Busch Stadium

It's fitting that St. Louis' baseball stadium is named for August A. Busch Jr. For it was Busch's foresight that led to the Cardinals' relocating to downtown St. Louis in the mid-1960s and a renaissance of sorts for the Gateway to the West.

In the years after the original Busch Stadium opened in 1966 — the same year in which the Cardinals held off the Atlanta Braves for a 4-3 win in the 12th inning of the first game ever played in the ballpark — St. Louis began to bloom. New office buildings, hotels, shopping complexes and other facilities now surround the stadium.

And rightfully so, since the Cards have been a constant in the world of baseball. The team won the World Series in 1982 and has traveled any number of times to the playoffs. And who will ever forget players like Ozzie Smith? Arguably one of the most memorable athletes to call Busch Stadium home, Smith was a defensive wizard who often performed backflips while running out to his shortstop position.

Delaware North was invited to be on "the team" as well when a new and improved Busch Stadium opened in 2006. Inspired by the new ballpark, the St. Louis Cardinals promptly went out and again won the World Series. They tallied a season record of 83-78 before downing the Detroit Tigers in five games.

Having picked up a title in its first year of existence, is there more Busch Stadium can do to improve upon its rookie season? Perhaps not. Still, the venue remains committed to giving every fan who steps in the stadium a chance to experience Cardinals baseball at its best.

Tomato Jam

Simple is beautiful. Those words will ring true for anyone who creates this recipe. Great as a spread for virtually any type of bread or cracker, this jam is simply wonderful.

Prep time: 20 minutes
Cook time: 40 minutes
Yields: 4 cups

1/4 cup olive oil

1 finely diced red onion

1/4 cup minced ginger

1 cup minced garlic

3 (8-ounce) cans diced tomatoes

1 cup red wine vinegar

1 1/2 cups honey

1 cup brown sugar

1/2 tablespoon dry ginger

1/2 tablespoon cinnamon

Salt to taste

Ground black pepper to taste

Heat oil in a 2-quart saucepan. Add red onion and cook for 5 minutes or until onions are translucent. Add ginger and garlic, and cook for an additional 5 minutes, keeping heat low so mixture doesn't brown.

Add tomatoes and vinegar and bring to a simmer for approximately 5 minutes.

Add honey and brown sugar. Simmer for 30 minutes or until juice has a thick, syrup-like consistency. Add ginger and cinnamon, and salt and pepper to taste. Cool before eating.

Easy to grow, versatile and bursting with flavor, tomatoes are the most popular garden fruit in the United States. However, if they come off the vine too soon, don't worry. Tomatoes produce ethylene as they ripen, so placing them in a closed brown paper bag will allow them to ripen faster.

Buttermilk Cheddar Drop Scones

An extraordinary beginning to any special meal, these scones are next to impossible to put down. Easy to make and full of great flavor, they are simply a culinary treat.

Prep time: 15 minutes
Cook time: 15 minutes
Yields: 26 (2-ounce) scones

3 3/4 cups all-purpose flour	1 teaspoon salt	10 tablespoons softened butter
5 1/2 tablespoons granulated sugar	1 cup buttermilk	1/4 cup shredded cheddar cheese
4 1/2 teaspoons baking powder	2 eggs	1/4 cup minced chives

Preheat oven to 350° F and lightly grease a baking sheet.

Mix flour, sugar, baking powder and salt in a bowl. Mix buttermilk and eggs in a separate bowl.

Using an electric mixer with a paddle attachment, combine flour mixture and softened butter on a low speed until mixture resembles a coarse meal. (Avoid mixing to a smooth consistency.)*

Gradually add the buttermilk/egg mixture. Mix on low until all ingredients are just incorporated. Fold in cheese and chives.

Using a spoon, drop 1-inch scoops of dough onto the greased baking sheet. (Note: An ice cream scoop (size 24) works well for this step.)

Bake for 12 to 15 minutes or until scones are a light golden brown. Serve warm with butter or tomato jam.

*If an electric mixer is not available, mix ingredients by hand. Do not use a whisk, as this tends to overmix the dough.

We owe a debt of gratitude to the British for sharing scones with the world. Closely resembling an American biscuit, scones are often filled with raisins, currants, dates or cheese and are sold at tea shops, bakeries and markets throughout Britain.

Pecan Chicken Satay
with Thai Peanut Sauce

A satay is a dish consisting of strips of marinated meat on skewers that are dipped in peanut sauce. Busch Stadium chefs took the liberty of adding a few twists to the recipe, thus creating a treat that's extra special.

Prep time: 10 minutes
Cook time: 4 minutes (per batch)
Yields: 32 skewers

2 quarts vegetable oil

8 (4-ounce) chicken breasts

32 bamboo skewers

1 cup pecans

3/8 cup brown sugar

Salt to taste

Ground black pepper to taste

1/2 cup cornstarch

3 whipped eggs

1 cup Thai Peanut Sauce (see below)

Heat vegetable oil in a deep fryer or medium cast-iron skillet to 350° F.

Trim chicken breasts of any fat and cut each one into four equal strips. Skewer each strip.

Make breading by finely chopping pecans with a food processor and mixing with brown sugar, salt and pepper.

Dust each skewer with cornstarch, then dip in egg wash and roll in pecan breading.

Deep fry for 3 to 4 minutes as close to service as possible.

Serve with Thai Peanut Sauce (see below).

Thai Peanut Sauce

Prep time: 5 minutes
Cook time: 10 minutes
Yields: 2 cups

2 tablespoons sesame oil

2 tablespoons finely minced garlic

1/4 cup soy sauce

1 cup coconut milk

1 tablespoon fish sauce*

1 cup peanut butter

1/2 tablespoon red pepper flakes

1 bias-cut green onion

Heat sesame oil in a small saucepan over low-medium heat. Add garlic, soy sauce, coconut milk and fish sauce. Gently cook 4 to 5 minutes or until garlic is translucent. Gradually heat without boiling.

Whisk in peanut butter, red pepper flakes and green onions.

Use as a dipping sauce.

A Thai fish sauce, available in the Asian section of your grocery store, is ideal in this recipe.

Portobello Fries
with Lemon Garlic Aioli

There's no documented answer for how the Portobello mushroom got its name. Some believe it comes from Portobello Road in London, while others think it has something to do with a television show called "Portobello." Regardless, after guests try this dish, they'll be calling it delicious.

Prep time: 1 hour, 20 minutes
Cook time: 5 minutes
Yields: 4 to 6 servings

1 quart oil for frying	1 tablespoon chopped, fresh thyme	1 cup all-purpose flour
4 medium Portobello mushrooms	1/4 cup olive oil for marinating	2 cups Italian breadcrumbs
(stems and black gills removed)	4 eggs	1/2 cup grated Romano cheese
1 tablespoon minced garlic	3 tablespoons water	Lemon Garlic Aioli for dipping (see below)

Preheat oil in a deep fryer to 350° F.

Slice mushrooms in 1/2-inch wedges. Marinate for 1 hour in the minced garlic, fresh thyme and just enough olive oil to coat.

Mix eggs with water to form an egg wash.

Season flour with salt and pepper and mix the breadcrumbs with the Romano cheese. Place the Portobello strips first in the flour, followed by the egg wash and lastly, the breadcrumbs.

Carefully drop the fries into the hot oil. Fry for 4 minutes or until fries are golden brown and crisp. Remove from oil and place on a plate lined with paper towels to absorb excess oil.

Lemon Garlic Aioli

Prep time: 5 minutes
Cook time: None
Yields: 1 1/2 cups

Juice of 1 lemon	1 cup mayonnaise
1/4 cup chopped parsley	Salt to taste
1 teaspoon minced garlic	Ground black pepper to taste

Combine all ingredients in a small bowl and adjust seasonings with salt and pepper.

Reserve under refrigeration until needed.

If not for cold Belgian winters, French fries may never have come into existence. In the late 1600s, poor inhabitants of Belgium would fry small fish for their meals, but when the rivers froze, they were left hungry. As a result, they began cutting potatoes lengthwise and frying them in oil as a tasty substitute.

St. Louis Hand-Rolled Pretzels

While many ballparks purchase pre-made pretzels, the Busch Stadium culinary team takes the time to carefully hand roll each pretzel that's sold. Trust us, you'll taste the difference.

Prep Time: 1 hour (30 minutes to proof)
Cook time: 12 to 15 minutes
Yields: 4 large pretzels

1 cup warm water (110° F)	2 teaspoons kosher salt	1/4 cup melted butter
1 tablespoon dry yeast	1 cup hot water	2 tablespoons kosher salt
3 1/2 cups all-purpose flour	2 teaspoons baking soda	
1/4 cup brown sugar	1 egg beaten with 1 teaspoon water (egg wash)	

Preheat oven to 425° F.

Mix water and yeast well, and set aside for 5 minutes.

Attach a dough hook to a stand mixer and add flour, sugar and salt to the mixing bowl. Mix for 3 minutes.

Divide dough into four equal parts. Roll each into a rope 6 inches long by 1/2 inch wide. Make into a pretzel shape (or any shape desired) and place on a baking pan lined with parchment paper. Set aside and allow to proof for 30 minutes.

Meanwhile, mix 1 cup of hot water with baking soda, and pour into a spray bottle. Spray each pretzel. Then brush each one with the egg wash.

Place pretzels in the oven and bake for 12 to 15 minutes or until brown. Brush warm pretzels with melted butter and sprinkle with salt.

St. Louis Toasted Ravioli

When Chef Terry Hill at Oldani's Restaurant on The Hill in St. Louis accidentally dropped some freshly made raviolis in breadcrumbs and decided to deep fry them, he probably didn't think he was creating a recipe that would forever be associated with his city. However, some 60 years later, Toasted Ravioli remains a St. Louis staple. While it's earned a following in other parts of the country and undergone a few tweaks and twists, St. Louis continues to claim it as its own.

Prep time: 15 minutes
Cook time: 10 minutes
Yields: 6 (3-piece) servings

1/4 cup whole milk	1/2 teaspoon kosher salt	2 tablespoons grated Parmesan cheese
1 large egg	1/2 package defrosted meat or cheese ravioli	1 tablespoon chopped parsley
1 cup Italian breadcrumbs	1 quart vegetable oil (for frying)	1 (16-ounce) jar marinara sauce

Combine milk and egg in a small bowl. Place breadcrumbs and salt in a separate, shallow bowl. Dip ravioli in milk mixture and coat with breadcrumbs.

In a medium saucepan, heat marinara sauce over medium heat until bubbling. Reduce heat and let the sauce simmer.

Pour 2 inches of oil into a large, heavy kettle or an electric deep fryer. Heat oil over medium heat to 350° F or until a small amount of breading sizzles and turns brown. Fry ravioli a few at a time, 1 minute on each side or until golden brown. Drain on paper towels.

Sprinkle with Parmesan cheese and parsley. Serve immediately with hot marinara sauce.

Chicken Slider

The original slider packed all the taste of a hamburger into a smaller size. The same stands true for a welcome variation: the chicken slider. These miniature sandwiches are as delicious as they are versatile, working as appetizers or as entrées. Either way, they won't disappoint.

Prep time: 20 minutes
Cook time: 10 minutes
Yields: 10 (2-ounce) patties

4 large chicken breasts	1 tablespoon finely minced garlic	Ground black pepper to taste
1 tablespoon parsley	1/4 cup finely diced yellow onion	1/4 cup Italian breadcrumbs
1 1/2 teaspoons fresh oregano leaves	1 egg	
1 1/2 teaspoons fresh thyme	Salt to taste	

Preheat grill to medium-high.

Roughly chop chicken. Mix with finely chopped herbs.

Chop onions and garlic, and add to chicken. Using a food processor, create ground meat.

Blend egg thoroughly and mix with salt and pepper. Add to chicken mix along with breadcrumbs. Mix thoroughly. Make a sample slider. Grill for 3 to 4 minutes on each side. Taste and adjust seasoning.

Form and cook remaining patties in the same manner. Serve on small dinner rolls or freshly baked bread.

Edward Jones Dome

Q: *Which U.S. venue was the site of the largest indoor gathering in the country's history?*

A: In 1999, Edward Jones Dome, the home of the NFL's St. Louis Rams, held the more than 104,000 people who came to participate in a Mass celebrated by Pope John Paul II.

The bit of trivia is evidence of the ingenious and imaginative design behind the stadium. In addition to serving as the home base of the Rams, it is one of the most versatile live entertainment venues in the world.

To wit: The venue can easily be transformed from a football field to exhibition hall, and its physical connection to the America's Center Convention Complex easily facilitates the latter. Still, it's stayed true to its original design of being a football center, setting the stage for games numerous and noteworthy.

In 1999, the Dome saw the Rams defeat the Minnesota Vikings 49-37 and then the Tampa Bay Buccaneers 11-6 to earn a spot in the Super Bowl. The Rams then went on to win the 1999 Super Bowl by a score of 23-16 over the Tennessee Titans to bring the Vince Lombardi Trophy back home. The venue was also the site of the Rams' 2001 NFC Championship game win over the Green Bay Packers.

Now fully equipped with The Rams Club and the Budweiser Brew House, Edward Jones Dome is poised to continue pleasing fans at football games and big-time events for years to come.

127

Fresh Baked Apple Dumplings with Maple Syrup Sauce

Apple dumplings create a dilemma. The flavorful aroma will have your guests longing to eat them, but the visual appeal will make you want to leave them untouched. The easy answer: Display them during dinner and dig in for dessert.

Prep time: 10 minutes
Cook time: 25 minutes
Yields: 6 servings

FOR THE SIMPLE SYRUP

2 cups water

1 cup granulated sugar

1 cinnamon stick (optional)

1 clove (optional)

1 teaspoon vanilla extract

FOR THE DUMPLINGS

3 Delicious apples

1 sheet thawed puff pastry

3 eggs, beaten

3 tablespoons granulated sugar

3 tablespoons brown sugar

2 teaspoons cinnamon

2 tablespoons softened, unsalted butter

1/2 cup maple syrup

Combine the simple syrup ingredients in a medium saucepan. Place over medium heat and bring to a gentle simmer.

Peel, halve and core the apples. Place in lightly simmering simple syrup and parcook for 8 to 10 minutes or until apples begin to tenderize. Doneness can be checked by inserting a toothpick or bamboo skewer into the center of one of the apples. Remove and chill the apples in the poaching liquid.

Preheat oven to 350° F.

Cut the puff pastry into six equal squares. Brush the sheet of puff pastry with some of the egg wash and sprinkle generously with granulated sugar, brown sugar and cinnamon.

Mix most of the remaining sugar and cinnamon with the softened butter, reserving enough of the cinnamon-sugar mixture to sprinkle on the top of the dumplings. Place a dollop of the butter mixture in the center of each square.

Place an apple half, flat side down, on top of the butter. Cut four diagonal lines from where the apple ends to the four corners of the puff pastry.

Take the first piece of each corner and fold to the top of the apple, forming a star or a pinwheel. Seal the pastry at the top of the apple and brush again with the egg wash. Sprinkle some cinnamon and sugar on the top of the apple dumpling.

Place dumplings in the oven. While they are baking, heat the maple syrup in a small pan until warm.

When dumplings are golden brown (after 12 to 15 minutes of baking), remove them from the oven and place on a plate. Brush hot maple syrup on them. If desired, leftover syrup can be used for dipping each bite.

Note: Vanilla ice cream is an ideal accompaniment to the warm dumplings.

Chicken Curry Wrap

Sportservice chefs often go the extra mile to make a recipe truly special. A perfect example of this is the Chicken Curry Wrap. While chicken wraps are tasty in their own right, our chefs take the time to toss in the flavorful curry spice and create a unique entrée.

Prep time: 15 minutes
Yields: 2 servings

2 (6-ounce) cooked, smoked chicken breasts

2 (12-inch) herb spinach wraps

1/4 cup honey

1 1/2 cups sour cream (can add more if you like)

1/4 cup raisins

1/2 cup chopped celery

1/4 cup seedless red grapes, cut lengthwise

1/2 tablespoon curry powder

Salt to taste

Dice chicken breasts into medium pieces. Place honey, sour cream, raisins, celery and grapes in a bowl and mix. Add curry powder and salt into the bowl as well.

Lay herb wraps out flat. Place one-half of all ingredients in the middle of each wrap and roll the wraps lengthwise.

Cut wraps on a bias. Serve cold.

SAN DIEGO

PETCO Park

When San Diego Padre fans head to PETCO Park to watch their team, they have the option of whiling away the day. With so much to do at the ballpark, it's easy to get lost in this beautiful downtown venue.

An architect's dream, PETCO Park celebrates the Pacific Ocean and San Diego, the city often acclaimed for its near-perfect weather. Although new, it is filled with charm like the historic Western Metals Building that serves as the venue's cornerstone, and remarkable sight lines that allow fans to take in spectacular views of downtown and even Balboa Park, home of the San Diego Zoo.

PETCO Park is a state-of-the-art stadium in its own right. Its designers pulled restaurants, offices and other structures away from the seating bowl in order to ensure the ballpark's concourses are open not only to the playing field but also to the surrounding city. A park-in-the-park behind the home run fence in center field makes the big-league entertainment affordable and enjoyable for all. Families picnic during games and kids scamper up and down the hill.

Tony Gwynn no longer runs the bases for the Padres, but the corridor outside and the Padres of today pay tribute to the brand of baseball he stands for. The team has won more than 80 games each season since 2004 when PETCO Park first opened its gates, advancing twice to the National League Division Series.

Dining options like the SONY Dugout Club and numerous other restaurants, including the diminutive Little Friars' Shack for kids, offer unbeatable culinary choices as well.

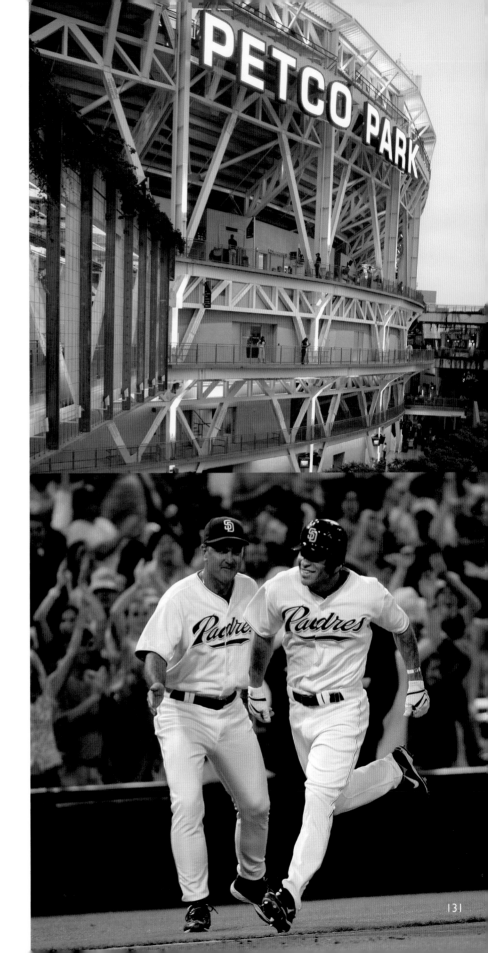

Southwestern Salad

A zesty, fun salad for any casual dinner party, PETCO Park's Southwestern Salad mixes field greens, shredded cheddar, roasted corn, black beans, avocado and tomatillo vinaigrette for one dynamic taste.

Prep time: 15 minutes
Cook time: 5 minutes
Yields: 4 servings

2 quarts vegetable oil

4 (12-inch) tortilla shells

8 ounces field greens

1 1/2 cups Roasted Tomatillo Vinaigrette (see below)

1/2 cup shredded cheddar cheese

1/2 cup roasted corn

1/2 cup black beans

3 finely diced Roma tomatoes

1 peeled, seeded and julienned avocado

Heat oil to 350° F in a deep fryer.

Carefully place a tortilla in hot oil. When it starts to bubble, press down on the tortilla with a slotted spoon or tongs until the shell is crisp and golden brown.

Remove the tortilla and let it drain on paper towels. Repeat the process with remaining tortilla shells. Set aside until needed. Toss field greens in a large bowl with enough Roasted Tomatillo Vinaigrette to coat the greens. Place on the fried tortilla shells and garnish with the remaining ingredients.

Serve immediately.

Roasted Tomatillo Vinaigrette

Prep time: 15 minutes
Cook time: 15 minutes
Yields: 1 1/2 cups

2 large tomatillos

1/3 cup apple cider vinegar

1/4 cup picked and chopped cilantro

1 tablespoon minced red onions

1 tablespoon granulated sugar

2/3 cup olive oil

Juice from 1 lime

Salt to taste

Ground black pepper to taste

Preheat oven to 350° F.

Place tomatillos on a baking sheet and roast for 15 minutes. Set aside and allow to cool.

Place vinegar, cilantro, red onions and sugar in a bar blender and purée. With the blender running, slowly drizzle in the oil to form an emulsion. Add the lime juice and season to taste with salt and pepper.

Diego Dog

Somewhat different from other stadium hot dogs, the Diego Dog takes cabbage and mixes it with salsa as a topping for the frankfurter that sits in a hoagie roll. Ideal for Padres fans, it's a distinctive taste derived from the Southwest.

Prep time: 10 minutes
Cook time: 5 minutes
Yields: 4 servings

4 jumbo all-beef hot dogs

4 hoagie rolls

1 cup shredded cabbage

4 tablespoons diced tomatoes

1 cup purchased salsa (any brand)

4 teaspoons grain mustard

Preheat grill to high. Place hot dogs on the grill and cook 4 to 5 minutes or until they are caramelized. Place each one in a hoagie roll. Top with shredded cabbage, diced tomatoes, salsa and mustard.

Fish Tacos

San Diego's own take on the taco: Crisp strips of fried fish fill up a tortilla and pop with a combination of extreme flavors. Padres fans eat these up at a rapid pace from the first pitch right through the seventh-inning stretch. Bring home a little West Coast flavor with this recipe and help your favorite fans root for their team.

Prep time: 10 minutes
Cook time: 10 minutes
Yields: 4 servings

1 cup finely shredded cabbage

1 cup iceberg or other crisp, shredded lettuce

12 warmed corn tortillas

2 pounds breaded cod fish nuggets
  (bake or fry according to directions)*

1 1/4 cups Lime Aioli (see below)

1 cup medium-spice salsa verde

1 cup finely shredded Monterey jack cheese

1/2 cup diced tomatoes
  (remove pulp and seeds prior to dicing or
  substitute 1 4-ounce can of diced tomatoes)

Combine shredded cabbage and lettuce.

Place a corn tortilla on a plate, centering 3 to 4 fish nuggets (depending on size).

Add 1 tablespoon aioli and a handful of shredded mix. Add 1 tablespoon of salsa verde and 2 tablespoons of shredded cheese.

Garnish with a few diced tomato pieces and fold.

*Mahi-mahi also works well.

Lime Aioli

Prep time: 5 minutes
Yields: 1 1/4 cups

1 cup mayonnaise

1/4 cup milk

Juice of 1 lime

12 drops Sri Racha hot lime sauce

Mix all together and keep chilled until needed.

Prosciutto and Spinach Rotol

"Prosciutto" is the Italian word for ham, and in the English language, it is used to refer to cured ham. The process for making prosciutto can take anywhere from nine to 18 months. With this rich recipe, all of that time is put to good use.

Prep time: 15 minutes
Cook time: 1 hour, 20 minutes
Yields: 8 servings

1 (3-pound) flank steak, butterflied lengthwise	1/3 cup grated Parmesan cheese	1/4 cup olive oil
4 to 5 slices thinly sliced prosciutto	Salt to taste	1 (28-ounce) can drained and diced
1 cup stemmed, fresh baby spinach	Ground black pepper to taste	San Marzano tomatoes
1/3 cup seasoned breadcrumbs	2 cloves finely minced garlic	1/4 cup dry white wine

Preheat oven to 375° F.

Open flank steak and lightly pound it. Add a single layer of prosciutto, followed by a layer of spinach. Sprinkle breadcrumbs, Parmesan cheese, salt, pepper and garlic on top.

Pull filling toward you while rolling in order to prevent stuffing from spilling out. Tie with butcher's twine. Brush outside of roll with olive oil and sprinkle with salt and pepper.

In a large skillet, heat enough olive oil to coat the bottom of the skillet and brown the beef roll, turning every 4 minutes so that the roll is browned on all sides. Remove and place in a deep baking pan. Place in the preheated oven.

Immediately drain the excess fat from the skillet used to brown the beef roll. After ensuring the skillet is still hot, carefully pour tomatoes in, stirring and scraping the sides of the skillet while mixing the tomatoes with the beef drippings. Check seasoning and adjust as needed. Simmer for 10 minutes. Raise the heat and add wine. Allow to bubble briskly for 3 to 4 minutes.

Remove beef from the oven and pour the prepared tomato sauce over the beef roll. Allow to bake 40 to 50 minutes or until internal temperature is 145° F, basting every 15 minutes.

When done, remove and let rest for 10 minutes. Remove butcher's twine before slicing.

For added zestiness, squeeze one-half of a lemon over roll while basting.

Veal Cutlet Bruschetta Hoagie

Why add anything to a perfect veal cutlet? Because the bruschetta spread enhances the flavor that much more! This sandwich is a delightful and unexpected addition to any tailgating party.

Prep time: 30 minutes
Cook time: 12 minutes
Yields: 4 servings

1 pound thinly sliced and pounded veal eye	2 beaten eggs	1 cup bruschetta (see below)
Salt to taste	1 cup Italian breadcrumbs	6 finely minced basil leaves
Ground black pepper to taste	1/2 cup olive oil	
1/2 cup all-purpose flour	4 sliced hoagie rolls	

Season veal lightly with salt and pepper.

Dredge veal in flour, then eggs, followed by breadcrumbs. Shake off excess.

Heat olive oil in a large skillet over medium-high heat. Carefully place veal into pan and brown each side for 4 minutes. Remove from oil and place on a plate lined with paper towels to absorb excess oil.

Lightly toast hoagie rolls.

Slice veal lengthwise and place in hoagie, topping with bruschetta.

Sprinkle minced basil on top.

Bruschetta

Prep time: 5 minutes
Yields: 1 cup

1/2 cup finely diced roasted red peppers	2 tablespoons olive oil	1 tablespoon chopped basil
2 seeded and finely diced Roma tomatoes	1 tablespoon white balsamic vinegar	Salt to taste
1/4 cup finely diced provolone cheese	1 tablespoon chopped parsley	Ground black pepper to taste
1 clove finely minced garlic		

Mix all ingredients together. Add salt and pepper to taste. Refrigerate.

STOCKTON

Stockton Arena

Capt. Charles Weber was not alone in his pursuit of California gold in the mid-1800s. What set him apart, however, was his realization that serving the needs of fortune seekers was an infinitely more worthwhile – and profitable – endeavor. So, the German immigrant purchased a parcel of land and founded the city of Stockton in what is now the San Joaquin Valley.

Fast forward a century and a half to 2005. The same town opens Stockton Arena, a top-of-the-line facility that has quickly gained acclaim as a host for big-time concerts and events. That's no small accomplishment in a state that is rich with big-time collegiate and professional sports teams, not to mention famous venues. But as the home of Major League Soccer's California Cougars; the Stockton Lightning, an Arena Football League team; and the Stockton Thunder, an ECHL National Division Franchise, Stockton is holding its own. And then some.

An integral piece of a waterfront entertainment center that includes Banner Island Ballpark, home of minor league baseball's Stockton Ports, Stockton Arena gives fans the thrill of being close to the action in a relaxed, family-friendly atmosphere. Equipped with the Comcast Club and fully catered suites, it's also a fine place to dine. When it's filled – as it often is – the arena can give 11,800 people one of the greatest live entertainment experiences possible.

Which just goes to show you Weber was right. There's gold in Stockton.

Fried Asparagus
with Wasabi Dipping Sauce

It only makes sense that Stockton, the home of the annual Asparagus Festival, has such a wonderful asparagus dish. This recipe adds the Wasabi Dipping Sauce, using it to enhance the arena's popular side dish.

Prep time: 15 minutes
Cook time: 10 minutes
Yields: 4 to 6 servings

2 quarts vegetable oil (for frying)	Kosher salt to taste	Cornstarch as needed
1 cup commercial tempura batter mix	Ground black pepper to taste	20 stalks medium, green asparagus
3/4 cup ice-cold water	1/4 cup bock beer (or your favorite dark beer)	Wasabi Dipping Sauce (see below)

Preheat oil in a deep fryer to 350° F.

Measure ice-cold water into mixing bowl. Sprinkle in tempura batter. Add salt, pepper and beer. Mix until lumps disappear.

Remove the woody part of asparagus bottoms and peel halfway up the stems.

Place cornstarch in a large bowl. Dredge asparagus in cornstarch and dip in tempura batter.

Carefully drop into the hot oil. Deep fry to golden brown. Remove from oil and place on a plate lined with paper towels. Adjust seasonings.

Serve hot with Wasabi Dipping Sauce.

Wasabi Dipping Sauce

Prep time: 5 minutes
Yields: 1 1/4 cups

1 cup mayonnaise	3 teaspoons lemon juice	Salt to taste
4 teaspoons soy sauce	3 teaspoons wasabi paste (wasabi powder mixed	Ground black pepper to taste
2 1/2 teaspoons granulated sugar	with just enough water to form a paste)	

Mix all of the ingredients and season with salt and pepper. Reserve under refrigeration until needed.

Seafood Crêpes
with Champagne Cream

Stockton Sportservice Chef Richard Valerio insists this is one of his favorite dishes to create and enjoy. Take the time to prepare it and you'll soon see why.

FOR THE CRÊPES
Prep time: 7 minutes
Cook time: 20 minutes
Yields: 4 servings

2 tablespoons butter

1/2 cup all-purpose flour

1/2 tablespoon salt

1/2 cup plus 3 tablespoons milk

1/4 cup water

2 large eggs

2 tablespoons sugar

FOR THE SAUCE
Prep time: 20 minutes
Cook time: 25 minutes
Yields: 1 quart

2 tablespoons butter

1/4 cup finely diced onions*

1/4 cup finely diced carrots*

1/4 cup finely diced celery*

1 1/2 teaspoons minced shallots

1 tablespoon minced garlic cloves

1 bay leaf

1 cup white wine

1 tablespoon lobster base
  (can substitute purchased shrimp paste)

1 cup shrimp stock or water

2 cups whipping cream

3/4 cup champagne

1 1/2 tablespoons cornstarch

Salt to taste

Ground black pepper to taste

Diced fresh chives for garnish

FOR THE FILLING
Prep time: 10 minutes
Cook time: 5 to 7 minutes
Yields: Filling for 4 servings

2 teaspoons unsalted butter

8 ounces uncooked lobster meat

8 ounces bay shrimp**

8 ounces quartered sea scallops

1 tablespoon chopped garlic

8 ounces oyster mushrooms

1/4 cup champagne sauce (see next page)

1 cup diced Roma tomatoes

1 tablespoon chopped green onion

Salt to taste

Ground black pepper to taste

*Dicing should yield 1/4-inch pieces.

**Approximately 70 to 90 per pound.

For the crêpes

Melt butter over low heat. Cool slightly.

Mix flour, salt, milk and water. Add eggs. Finish with butter and allow to rest for 20 minutes.

Heat a small nonstick sauté or crêpe pan over medium heat. Add a small amount of butter or cooking spray.

Pour batter in pan, tilting pan until batter covers the bottom of the pan with an even layer.

Cook until lightly browned. Turn over and cook until firm.

For the champagne sauce

Heat butter in a 2-quart saucepan. Sauté all vegetables in butter for 5 minutes or until translucent.

Add 1 cup white wine and reduce by half. Add lobster base and shrimp stock. Simmer for 5 minutes. Strain the mixture with an extra-fine strainer and return to saucepan.

Add whipping cream and simmer for 10 minutes. Add champagne.

Dissolve the cornstarch in water.

Bring sauce to a boil and add cornstarch. Cook for 1 to 2 minutes or until sauce thickens. Season with salt and pepper.

For the filling

Heat sauté pan over medium-high heat. Add 2 teaspoons of unsalted butter. Add seafood, garlic and oyster mushrooms.

Cook for 3 minutes or until the seafood is cooked through.

Add champagne sauce to coat. Fold in diced tomatoes and green onions.

Season with salt and pepper to taste.

To serve

Fill crêpes with seafood mixture and roll individually. Place two crêpes on each plate, dressing with hot champagne sauce. Add remaining seafood filling on top. Garnish with fresh chives.

TAMPA

St. Pete Times Forum

Maybe warm ocean breezes and tropical drinks don't conjure up images of hockey. But that did little to deter the National Collegiate Athletic Association (NCAA). It will bring the 2012 Frozen Four to the St. Pete Times Forum.

The message? Don't be fooled by Tampa…it's a hockey town.

Lightning fans have been saying that all along, especially after the NHL franchise captured the Stanley Cup in 2004. The team defeated the Calgary Flames 4-3 in the Stanley Cup Finals, bringing sports' most iconic trophy home to Florida.

However, the St. Pete Times Forum is much more than a good place to play hockey. It also hosts the Tampa Bay Storm, an Arena Football League team. When it's not busy holding events for its home teams, the building is constantly being called upon to host other world-class events.

In 1999, for example, it welcomed the NHL All-Star Game, which saw hockey great Wayne Gretzky record a goal and two assists en route to earning MVP honors for the game. In 2003, the first- and second-round games of the NCAA Men's Basketball Tournament visited the St. Pete Times Forum, and in 2007, it was the host of the 2007 ACC Men's Basketball Tournament

Designers of the building thought they had a near-impossible task: Bring great hockey action to Florida. Now, more than a decade after its opening, the St. Pete Times Forum has proven itself more than capable.

Cuban Sandwich

A meat lover's dream come true, this regional sandwich calls for pork roast, ham and salami all smothered in cheese. Add Cuban bread, and you have a one-of-a-kind light meal everyone will enjoy.

Prep time: 15 minutes
Cook time: 5 minutes
Yields: 2 (8-inch) servings

1 loaf Cuban bread (or any rustic flat bread)	8 kosher dill pickle slices	4 ounces thinly sliced and shredded pork roast
1/4 cup spicy brown mustard	4 ounces thinly sliced Swiss cheese	2 ounces Genoa salami (optional)
1/4 cup mayonnaise	4 ounces thinly sliced ham	

Slice Cuban bread lengthwise.

Combine mustard and mayonnaise thoroughly. Spread mixture evenly on inside of bread.

Place pickle slices on bottom half of bread. Layer half of Swiss cheese over the pickle slices and set the rest aside.

Layer pork, ham and salami over Swiss cheese. Cover with remaining half of Swiss cheese and place top half of bread over the Swiss cheese.

Cut Cuban sandwich in half using a straight cut.

Place sandwiches in a heated sandwich press and apply moderate pressure.

Heat sandwiches for approximately 4 to 5 minutes or until sandwiches are hot and the cheese has melted.

Slice each sandwich in half diagonally and serve immediately.

Double-Decker Plant City Strawberry Shortcake

It would be sinful to let ripe, homegrown strawberries go to waste. This recipe ensures you never will again. A summer favorite made even better.

Prep time: 8 minutes
Yields: 6 servings

2 pints cleaned, fresh strawberries

2 tablespoons granulated sugar

1 tablespoon Grand Marnier

1 cup heavy whipping cream

1 tablespoon vanilla extract

2 tablespoons powdered sugar

1 (6" x 2" x 2") pound cake

Rinse strawberries, pat dry, slice and place in a medium bowl.

Coat half of the strawberries with granulated sugar and Grand Marnier, gently toss and allow to macerate in the refrigerator, preferably overnight. Reserve remaining strawberries for garnish.

Place the heavy cream in a small mixing bowl. Using an electric mixer, whip on high speed until slightly thick. Add vanilla extract and powdered sugar and continue to whip until light and fluffy.

Slice the pound cake lengthwise in two equal pieces and place the bottom portion on a large plate. Cover it with some of the strawberries, including juice. Spoon the whipped cream on top of the strawberries. Take the top of the pound cake and place on top of the whipped cream.

Cover the pound cake with remaining strawberries and pour juice over the top as desired. Spoon more whipped cream on top and garnish with reserved strawberries.

Boursin Roasted Beef Tenderloin
with Cherry Tomato and Red Onion Relish

The key to this recipe is the way that the Boursin cheese is applied at just the right time in order to create a memorable flavor. Paired with the tenderloin, these two key ingredients combine to create an extraordinary meal.

Prep time: 10 minutes
Cook time: 45 minutes
Yields: 12 servings

1 (3 1/2- to 4-pound) beef tenderloin*	1 tablespoon minced garlic	Ground white pepper to taste
2 tablespoons olive oil	Kosher salt to taste	1 wheel softened Boursin cheese

Preheat grill to medium-high and preheat oven to 350° F.

Trim the tenderloin and marinate it slightly with the olive oil, garlic, salt and pepper.

Place the tenderloin on the grill and sear it on all sides, but do not cook it.

Remove tenderloin from the grill, place in a roasting pan and cook 30 to 40 minutes or until internal temperature is 120° F.

When it's almost done, remove the tenderloin from the oven and rub it with Boursin cheese.

Place the tenderloin back in the oven for 10 to 15 minutes or until the internal temperature is 125° F. The finished tenderloin should be slightly browned and the cheese should be melted.

Remove roast from the oven and let rest for 10 minutes. Serve with Cherry Tomato and Red Onion Relish.

*Ask your meat cutter to make the tenderloin oven ready.

Cherry Tomato and Red Onion Relish

Prep time: 15 minutes
Yields: 2 cups or 8 servings

2 pints cleaned and quartered cherry tomatoes	1/4 cup olive oil	Kosher salt to taste
3/4 cup finely julienned red onions	1 tablespoon finely julienned fresh basil	Ground white pepper to taste
1/4 cup balsamic vinegar	1 tablespoon cleaned and finely chopped parsley	

Combine all ingredients in a medium bowl. Toss gently. Check seasonings. Adjust as needed.

Refrigerate for at least 2 hours. Serve cold.

TORONTO

Rogers Centre

There's little doubt Rogers Centre is one of the most innovative accomplishments in stadium entertainment history. Ever since it opened as the SkyDome June 3, 1989, it has achieved worldwide accolades for its retractable-roof design that allows domed and open-air events to be held within its confines.

The quality of sports that has been displayed by its residents, the Toronto Blue Jays and the Canadian Football League's Toronto Argonauts, has also been world-class. The Blue Jays won back-to-back World Series Championships in 1992 and 1993, while the Argonauts claimed the Grey Cup in 1991, 1996, 1997 and 2004.

And it's been the site of a number of I-wish-I-had-been-there moments, including Joe Carter's belting a three-run homer in the bottom of the ninth inning during game 6 of the 1993 World Series. That home run erased the 6-5 lead the Philadelphia Phillies held over Toronto, and gave the Jays a second world championship.

More than 2,000 events have been held at Rogers Centre since it opened and over 50 million people have visited the field. For four consecutive years, Rogers Centre was named stadium of the year by *Billboard, Amusement Business* and *Performance* magazines.

Still, Rogers Centre is most famous for its technological features. Fully equipped with a larger-than-life video board and dining options such as Sightlines Restaurant, an open-air dining area, the facility continues to be far ahead of its time. It is one of Toronto's top-three tourist attractions and has been the model for numerous city plans and stadium designs.

Developers even attached a hotel to the stadium, meaning guests of the 70 rooms with a view of the field can watch the Jays play ball, too.

Bocconcini Skewers

The word "bocconcini" is Italian for "mouthful." This definition describes not so much the size of each portion, but rather, the appeal of the dishes. With this recipe, it has a double meaning, referring to the mouthful of flavors that these skewers deliver and the type of cheese used in the recipe.

Prep time: 35 minutes
Cook time: None
Yields: 12 to 14 skewers

I pound drained, small bocconcini cheese

I bunch rinsed and drained basil leaves

I pound washed grape tomatoes

14 bamboo skewers

I cup Balsamic Drizzle (see below)

I cup Basil Oil (see below)

Sea salt to taste

Ground black pepper to taste

Wrap a piece of bocconcini with a basil leaf and place on a skewer followed by a grape tomato. Repeat two more times.

Arrange skewers on a white platter. Drizzle balsamic reduction and basil oil over each skewer and on edges of platter. Sprinkle with sea salt and ground black pepper.

Balsamic Drizzle

Prep time: 1 minute
Cook time: 15 minutes
Yields: 1 cup

I cup balsamic vinegar

I cup white balsamic vinegar

1/4 cup granulated sugar

Place in a small, nonreactive saucepan.

Reduce by half over medium heat until vinegar thickens.

Cool completely and reserve until needed.

Basil Oil

Prep time: 5 minutes
Cook time: 1 minute
Yields: 2 cups

Salt

3 cups fresh basil leaves

I cup extra-virgin olive oil

Place basil in salted boiling water and blanch for 10 seconds. Drain and shock in ice water for 1 minute. Drain again. Squeeze excess water and pat dry.

Place in a food processor or bar blender and pulse on high, slowly adding olive oil. Strain. Store covered.

Ahi Tuna Salad
with Vanilla Citrus Dressing

Blue Jays fans encounter a treat any time they find Ahi Tuna Salad on their menu. One of the most sought-after kinds of tuna, Ahi is found off of the shores of Hawaii, where its name means "fire." It's not surprising, then, that Toronto Sportservice chefs have come to expect this dish to be a hot item anytime it is featured at Rogers Centre.

Prep time: 8 minutes
Cook time: 7 minutes
Yields: 6 servings

1 teaspoon black peppercorns	1 tablespoon Hungarian paprika	2 peeled and segmented oranges
1/2 cup white sesame seeds	5 tablespoons Old Bay seasoning	Orange zest
1/2 cup black sesame seeds	2 tablespoons sesame seed oil	1/4 cup Vanilla Citrus Dressing (see below)
3 tablespoons seasoning salt	1 (8-ounce) fresh Ahi tuna steak	Pea or radish shoots for garnish
1 tablespoon kosher salt	3 cups spring salad mix (or mesclun)	

Heat a small sauté pan over medium-high heat. Roast peppercorns for 1 to 2 minutes. Remove from heat and crush.

Combine roasted and crushed peppercorns, sesame seeds, salts, paprika and Old Bay seasoning in a medium bowl and mix well.

Remove enough of the sesame seed mixture from the mixing bowl to coat tuna steak. (Unless it has come in contact with the tuna, remaining mixture can be stored in an airtight container for future use.)

Heat sesame seed oil in a medium cast-iron skillet over medium-high heat. Sear tuna for 5 minutes (rare). Remove from pan and refrigerate.

When ready to serve, remove tuna from the refrigerator and slice it on the bias.

Place salad greens on a platter. Place sliced tuna over greens in a fan pattern.

Place orange segments around platter and sprinkle orange zest lightly over the entire platter.

Top with 1/4 cup Vanilla Citrus dressing and garnish with fresh pea or radish shoots.

Vanilla Citrus Dressing

Prep time: 15 minutes
Yields: 2 cups

1 cup tangerine juice or marmalade	1/4 cup plus 2 tablespoons lime juice	Salt to taste
1/2 cup coconut milk	1/4 cup champagne vinaigrette	Ground black pepper to taste
1 vanilla bean (scrape pulp from inside of vanilla bean)	1/2 cup grape seed oil	

Place all ingredients (except oil, salt and pepper) in a food processor or bar blender and blend on high speed. Slowly add oil and continue blending until dressing is emulsified.

Add salt and pepper to taste.

Fig-Coated Lamb
with Roasted Red Pepper Spaetzle

The fig sauce that coats the lamb in this recipe is what makes it unique. Follow the instructions closely and you'll be able to create a dish your friends will request every time they visit.

Prep time: 45 minutes
Cook time: 1 hour, 10 minutes
Yields: 6 to 8 servings

FOR THE LAMB

1 cup chopped, dry figs

1 1/4 cups apple juice

2 tablespoons roasted garlic

Salt to taste

Ground black pepper to taste

2 racks cleaned Colorado lamb*

1/4 cup olive oil

FOR THE SPAETZLE

1 cup all-purpose flour

2 eggs

1/2 teaspoon ground nutmeg

1/2 teaspoon salt

1/4 cup milk

1/2 cup finely chopped roasted red peppers**

2 quarts hot water or chicken stock

1/4 cup butter

2 tablespoons chopped parsley

For the lamb

Preheat oven to 375° F.

Combine figs, apple juice, garlic, salt and pepper in a small saucepan and simmer for 20 minutes. Transfer mixture to a bar blender and blend well. Remove and allow to cool.

Season lamb racks with salt and pepper. Heat olive oil in a large skillet over medium-high heat. Sear lamb on all sides for 5 minutes. Place lamb racks in a medium roasting pan and rub fig mixture on them.

Place roasting pan in the preheated oven and cook for 20 minutes, until the internal temperature of the lamb is 125° F or until the dish reaches the temperature that you desire.

For the spaetzle

Using a stand mixer, combine flour, salt, nutmeg and peppers, and mix on low. Add one egg at a time, followed by the milk. Mix until smooth.

Heat water or chicken stock in a medium saucepan to a gentle boil.

Press dough through a holed sieve into the simmering water or stock in the saucepan. The dough will drop in the hot liquid, forming small, long dumplings. Cook for 8 to 10 minutes.

Gently pour liquid and spaetzle through a colander and drain spaetzle well.

When ready to serve the lamb, heat a small skillet over medium-high heat. Add butter and sauté spaetzle for 5 to 8 minutes or until light golden. Add parsley.

Note: Although the lamb is extremely flavorful on its own, a brown sauce or lamb jus would be a perfect complement.

*Ask your meat cutter to French-clean the bones for you.
**These can be purchased at your local market.

MEET OUR CHEFS

Rolf Baumann, CEC
Corporate Chef, Delaware North
 Companies Sportservice
Buffalo, New York

Best Sportservice memory?

"The 2005 Major League Baseball All-Star Game in
Detroit. We flew 14 chefs in from our other baseball
parks, and for three days, we cooked day and night.
For the first time in the company's history, we used
only interactive chef stations to take care of 900 guests.
And it worked beautifully. It was truly something to
see. On top of that, we hosted a 90th anniversary
party for Delaware North."

Favorite thing to cook?

"All food is fair game for me, but I especially enjoy
immersing myself in culture and learning about the
history of foods. It's always more rewarding to cook
items that are special to my guests. I found out early
in my career the more respect and attention you give
your cooking, the better your results will be."

Roland Henin, CMC
Corporate Chef, Delaware North Companies
Buffalo, New York

Best Delaware North moment?

"The 2006 Delaware North global managers meeting in
Orlando, where I received the Spirit to Soar Award
from Jerry Jacobs Jr. The honor was one of the
proudest moments of my career. It renewed my
commitment to make the Delaware North culinary team
the best in the business."

Best culinary advice?

"A simple and well-prepared dish is better than a
complicated one that is not made correctly."

Ricky Abrams
Sous Chef, Fifth Third Field
Dayton, Ohio

Best Sportservice moment?

"Opening day 2000 for Daytona baseball. I had been a
chef in health care, so my first time as a Sportservice
chef in a stadium was a new and different experience
for me."

Mark Angeles, CEC, CCA
Executive Chef, Soldier Field
Chicago, Illinois

Best Sportservice moment?

"Being part of the culinary team at Soldier Field the
year the Bears won the NFC championship."

Bill Bateman
Executive Chef, Reno-Sparks
 Convention Center
Reno, Nevada

Best Sportservice moment?

"Working the last World Series in St. Louis."

Eric Borgia, CCC
Executive Chef, PETCO Park
San Diego, California

Best Sportservice moment?

"The 2006 Superbowl in Detroit. The halftime act —
the Rolling Stones — was set up at Comerica Park.
We fed the Stones for four days while they prepared for
their show."

Conrad Courchesne
Executive Chef, Rexall Place and Telus Field
Edmonton, Alberta

Favorite thing to cook?

"Meats, overall, but especially lamb. I like racks (panko-crusted with Dijon and fresh herbs with a red wine reduction or barbecued). Meat is the base of most meals. Alberta has some of the BEST grain-fed beef, pork, lamb and exotic meats (bison, elk, muskook, caribou, etc.) in North America."

Tab Daulton, CEC
Executive Chef, HSBC Arena
Buffalo, New York

Best Sportservice moment?

"Cooking for the Buffalo Sabres during the Stanley Cup playoffs. Working closely with the training coach and earning his trust to provide whatever the team requested."

Kevin Doherty, CEC, CCA
Executive Chef, TD Banknorth Garden
Boston, Massachusetts

Best Sportservice moment?

"The 2004 Democratic National Convention."

Adrian Estrada
Executive Chef — Suites & Fine Dining,
  Dr Pepper Ballpark
Frisco, Texas

Favorite thing to cook?

"Barbecue brisket. I make all of the seasonings and barbecue sauce from scratch. Then I cook the meat slowly in the smoker. Not only is it great eating, it's always the start of lots of conversation and laughter between family and friends."

Stephen Gary Jr.
Executive Chef, St. Pete Times Forum
Tampa, Florida

Best Sportservice moment?

"Being involved in two of the Lightnings' four consecutive playoff runs. The atmosphere here was electric. We all felt like we were a part of the action and that every little thing we were doing was making a difference to the team."

Jeannie Goljenboom
Sous Chef, Wisconsin Exposition Center
  at State Fair Park
Milwaukee, Wisconsin

Best culinary advice?

"Eat dessert first so you'll have room for it!"

D. Christian Hipszer, CCC
Executive Chef, Ralph Wilson Stadium
Orchard Park, New York

Favorite thing to cook?

"Cooking is the easy part of my job. There are only seven ways (plus microwaving) to cook. Management is the real challenge. But my favorite foods would be seared tuna, domestic lamb and curried ostrich."

Pastor Jimenez
Executive Chef, Miller Park
Milwaukee, Wisconsin

Best Sportservice moment?

"Being part of the very talented culinary team at Soldier Field and having the opportunity to put my own culinary team together at Miller Park."

Jeramie Mitchell
Executive Chef, Busch Stadium
St. Louis, Missouri

Favorite thing to cook?

"I love to cook Mediterranean cuisine. The people of the Mediterranean cook with their emotions and their strong passion for food and life shines through. This is what cooking is all about. It doesn't matter if I'm cooking Asian, French or Mediterranean, I always cook in the manner of the Mediterranean people, letting my passion shine through my food."

James Major
Chef, Terrace Club, Progressive Field
Cleveland, Ohio

Best culinary advice?

"Pick and choose your kitchens wisely and don't worry about money or prestige. Worry about making great food and the rest will follow."

Jon Perrault
Director of Quality Assurance,
   Delaware North Companies Sportservice
Buffalo, New York

Best Sportservice moment?

"There are many, but the best one — hands down — was working with the Delaware North culinary team at the Australian Open and living in their world for 25 days. This is perhaps the most organized and quality-driven group of people I have ever seen. They are about the real experience of food and family. They share their time at the dinner tables and with each other (friends and family) and their focus is to work as one in the operation. They listened, they shared, they worked to make the customer experience their priority and it showed in every phase of the process. The quality of

product and the presentation that was maintained in serving more than 2,500 plated meals each day were absolutely amazing. The lessons learned there have been driven deep into my work ethic and I have tried to share many of those lessons with others."

Scott Pobuda, CCC
Executive Chef, Great American Ball Park
Cincinnati, Ohio

Favorite thing to cook?

"Anything over an open fire. I do a lot of camping and really like the challenge of making great meals without the luxury of a professional kitchen. Whole chickens and whole pigs are great when cooked on a spit. They get a great smoked flavor and are so juicy and tender that the meat falls off the bone."

Justin Scott
Sous Chef, Edward Jones Dome
St. Louis, Missouri

Favorite thing to cook?

"Bread. Baking bread is something that takes time and attention to detail. I love walking into a kitchen and smelling freshly baked bread coming out of the oven. There is nothing better in the world to me."

Mark Szubeczak, CCC
Executive Chef, Comerica Park
Detroit, Michigan

Best culinary advice?

"If you're a chef, never arrive early to a backyard barbecue!"

Chris Taylor
Sous Chef, O'Brien Field
Peoria, Illinois

Best culinary advice?

"Learn to do everything and work hard. It will get you far in life."

Cristobal Vazquez, CCA
Executive Chef, Rangers Ballpark in Arlington
Arlington, Texas

Best Sportservice moment?

"Catering the first Democratic convention post-9/11. There was unprecedented security and the largest collection of famous people I've ever seen."

Simon Roach
Executive Chef, Rogers Centre
Toronto, Ontario

Favorite thing to cook?

"Whole roast chicken. There's nothing so simple and satisfying. Crispy, salty, juicy and fresh. It will appeal to anyone from anywhere."

Robert Trevisanutto
Executive Chef, Wildwoods Convention Center
Wildwoods, New Jersey

Best culinary advice?

"Watch fewer food shows and get real experience in the field. Most people don't have a grasp on how difficult and rewarding the profession can be."

Richard Valerio
Executive Chef, Stockton Arena
Stockton, California

Best Sportservice moment?

"Catering a party at the La Jolla, California, home of Dick Freeman (president of the San Diego Padres). The menu and recipes for the dinner we served were featured in *San Diego Home/Garden*."

Special thanks to:

Beth Brown, CC
Sous Chef, The Ahwahnee
Yosemite, California

Favorite thing to cook?

"I recently moved from The BALSAMS in New Hampshire to The Ahwahnee in Yosemite. I love working with the fresh, local California produce and the cheeses we get from nearby creameries. They are fantastic. Wherever I am, I like to find out everything I can about the food."

INDEX OF RECIPES